総合英語

Let's Enjoy English

大学生のための総合英語

佐藤哲三
佐藤勇治
荒巻龍也
池田賢治
毛利史生

NAN'UN-DO

はじめに

　本書は、一般に敬遠されがちな英文法学習に重点を置きつつ英文読解もできるように効率的に編まれた総合英語教材です。高校を卒業して大学等に入学するまでに英語を6年以上も学んで来たのに、自信を持って英語を読んだり、書いたり、話したり、聴いたりすることができないと思う人が意外に多いのではないでしょうか。その大きな原因のひとつに英文法力不足を挙げることができるでしょう。英語に限らず、一般に外国語をある一定の期間で習得しようと思えば、発音や語彙の学習は勿論のこと、十分な文法学習が必要となります。中学、高校の6年間を振り返ってみてください。英文法を身に付ける時間は十分でしたか。学年が進行するにつれて英語嫌い、英文法嫌いが増えることから、不十分だったのではないかと思われます。この点を解決しなければこの先も思うように英語力が身につかないでしょう。「急がば回れ」です。まず、英文法の効率的な再学習を大学等での英語学習の出発点にして、会話力、聴解力、読解力、英作文力の向上につなげてください。

　本書では、基本英文法事項が18章に配分され、さらにそれぞれの文法事項が「基本」と「標準」に分けられていますので、誰もが、本書使用時点の文法力に応じた学習が可能です。

　本書の各章の構成は次のとおりです。各章とも「基本」（3頁）と「標準」（3頁）の二部構成です。一部・二部とも最初の頁がその章の文法事項の整理、2頁目がその文法事項の練習、最終頁が英文読解になっています。一部の「基本」は実用英語技能検定の3級・準2級レベルを、二部の「標準」は2級以上のレベルを想定して編まれています。それぞれの最初の「文法事項の整理」の頁は、例文を上から順に見ていくことにより、その文法事項のあらかたがわかるように配列されています。3頁目の英文は必ずしもその章で学習する文法事項に合致しているとは限りませんが、英検二次対策や速読にも利用できる内容になっています。

　最後に、本書の出版を快諾された南雲堂の南雲一範社長、編集実務の行き届いたご配慮をいただいた青木泰祐氏に心より感謝申し上げます。

　2007年　秋

著者一同

CONTENTS

はしがき …………………………………………………… 2
Chapter 1　文の種類 ……………………………………… 4
Chapter 2　動詞の種類と文型 …………………………… 10
Chapter 3　動詞（時制）………………………………… 16
Chapter 4　助動詞 ………………………………………… 22
Chapter 5　能動態と受動態 ……………………………… 28
Chapter 6　名詞 …………………………………………… 34
Chapter 7　冠詞と数詞 …………………………………… 40
Chapter 8　代名詞 ………………………………………… 46
Chapter 9　接続詞 ………………………………………… 52
Chapter 10　前置詞 ……………………………………… 58
Chapter 11　形容詞・副詞 ……………………………… 64
Chapter 12　比較 ………………………………………… 70
Chapter 13　不定詞 ……………………………………… 76
Chapter 14　分詞 ………………………………………… 82
Chapter 15　動名詞 ……………………………………… 88
Chapter 16　関係詞 ……………………………………… 94
Chapter 17　仮定法 ……………………………………… 100
Chapter 18　時制の一致・話法 ………………………… 106

Chapter 1-1
文の種類（1）

A 文の意味、内容による分類（1）

1. 平叙文
 1) Rome is the capital of Italy.
 2) I'm not an engineer.
 3) Mary gets up at six every morning.

2. 疑問文
 4) Is Rome a beautiful city?
 5) Do you have any money with you?
 6) Aren't the boys free now? No, they aren't.
 ※ 付加疑問文
 7) It is fine today, isn't it?
 8) Dick didn't go there, did he?

3. 命令文
 9) Look at the map of the city of Rome.
 10) Be quiet here.
 11) Don't speak Japanese in this room.

4. 感嘆文
 12) What a wonderful city Rome is!
 13) What an interesting book this is!
 14) How well she plays the piano!

B 文の構造による分類（1）

5. 単文
 15) I like dogs.
 16) There is a book on the desk.
 17) I sometimes go swimming with him.

6. 重文
 18) I am a nurse and she is a care worker.
 19) She went out, but I stayed at home.
 20) Start at once, and you will catch the bus.

7. 複文
 21) I know that he loves her.
 22) When I came home, Mother was cooking.
 23) If it is fine tomorrow, we will go on a picnic.

Exercises

A. 次の各文を（　　）内の指示に従って書き換えなさい。
1. Alice wants a little dog.（疑問文に）
2. Ben doesn't play the piano very well.（付加疑問のついた文に）
3. They went out after lunch.（否定文に）

B. 次の英文の下線部が答えとなるような疑問文を作りなさい。
1. <u>Ms. Smith</u> went to the department store yesterday.
2. Ms. Smith went <u>to the department store</u> yesterday.
3. Ms. Smith went to the department store <u>yesterday</u>.

C. 次の文を命令文にしなさい。
1. You are quiet here.
2. You don't mix these together.
3. You will be back here by eleven o'clock.

D. 次の英文を感嘆文に直しなさい。
1. That is a very amusing story.
2. You have very good pictures.
3. The athlete is running very fast.

E. 次の文は、単文、重文、複文のうちどれでしょうか。
1. I have an apple and some lemons in the box.
2. This is my cell phone and that is his electronic dictionary.
3. Though Mr. Tanaka lived in Brazil, he doesn't speak Portuguese well.
4. I think that Mother has gone shopping.
5. She went out, but I stayed at home.
6. She went to Hong Kong during the summer vacation.

F. 次の日本文を英文に直しなさい。
1. 私たちはほとんどの日曜日にサッカーをします。
2. あの背の高い紳士は誰ですか。
3. あなたは英語が大好きですよね。（付加疑問を用いて）

Exercises

G. 次の英文を読み、それに続く質問に英語で答えなさい。

Karaoke

Karaoke literally means "empty orchestra." Karaoke performers aren't accompanied by a band or orchestra. They sing along with background music that has been prerecorded without the words. Karaoke became popular in Japan in the 1970's, and the phenomenon quickly spread overseas. Today, it is one of the world's most popular forms of entertainment. When you ask young people what their hobby is, most answer karaoke, and adults love it, too.

Why is karaoke so popular? One reason is that such singing helps relieve stress. Another reason is that for a few minutes at least, karaoke performers can feel like professional singers. In addition, karaoke can improve communication between friends, colleagues, and family members.

Recently, the karaoke box has been catching on. This is a small room where a few friends can have the "box" all to themselves, and sing to their heart's content.

No.1 What do karaoke performers sing along with?

No.2 When did karaoke become popular in Japan?

No.3 What does karaoke help relieve?

No.4 How do karaoke performers feel when they sing?

Chapter 1-2

文の種類（2）

A 文の意味、内容による分類（2）

1. 平叙文
1) She had a good sleep last night.
2) Tom and Jerry weren't at home then.
3) He didn't go to school yesterday.

2. 疑問文
4) Is Mr. Suzuki here on business or for pleasure?
5) Won't you enter the museum? Yes, I will.
6) What is the use of talking to him? = It's no use talking to him.

3. 命令文
7) Don't be afraid of making mistakes.
8) Tell me what time the train leaves.
9) Let me know where he lives.

4. 感嘆文
10) How wonderful a city Rome is!
11) What interesting books these are!
12) What a shame!

B 文の構造による分類（2）

5. 単文
13) Why is he so angry with me?
14) He is tall enough to touch the ceiling.
15) Walking along the street, I met a friend of mine.

6. 重文
16) Get up early, or you will miss the train.
17) She was in poor condition, so she couldn't run fast.
18) It'll rain this evening, for the barometer is falling.

7. 複文
19) The book is so difficult that I can't read it.
20) He fell asleep while he was listening to music.
21) This is the village where I was born.

Exercises

A. 次の各文を（　　）内の指示に従って書き換えなさい。
1. He has been to America <u>three times</u>.（下線部を問う文に）
2. They went there <u>by train</u>.（下線部を問う文に）
3. Step aside.（付加疑問のついた文に）
4. Let's toss a coin to decide.（付加疑問のついた文に）
5. There's something wrong with this washer.（付加疑問のついた文に）
6. Dick has a very good bike.（感嘆文に）
7. The book is so difficult that I can't read it.（単文に）
8. Though it was cold, we didn't make a fire.（重文に）
9. Get up early, or you will miss the train.（複文に）

B. 次の各文が単文、重文、複文の何れであるか述べなさい。
1. He told me that he would go home.
2. Would you mind my opening the window?
3. There's no fear of his betraying me, for he is a reliable man.

C. 次の各文を単文に書き換えなさい。
1. Who came to see me while I was absent?
2. He studied hard so that he could pass the test.
3. If you turn to the right, you will find the school.

D. 次の各組の文が同じ意味になるように（　　）内に適語を入れなさい。
1. He is very tall, so he can reach the shelf.
   He is tall (　　) (　　) reach the shelf.
2. As he was poor, he could not go to college.
   His (　　) prevented him (　　) going to college.

E. 次の日本文を英文に直しなさい。
1. 「その件（matter）は我々にとって重要ではないのですか」「いいえ、重要です」
2. 彼は最善を尽したが失敗しました。（単文で）
3. すでに暗くなっていたが、彼らは仕事をやめませんでした。（重文で）
4. 彼が回復する見込みはありません。（複文で）

Exercises

F. 次の英文を読み、それに続く質問に英語で答えなさい。 3

The Survivor

What is the strongest living thing on earth? Is it a human being? Or is it the lion, the king of beasts? Or maybe the gorilla? No, none of these is correct. Believe it or not, the strongest living thing on earth is the cockroach. Fossils show us that cockroaches have been around for more than 300 million years. They were living on our planet long before the dinosaurs. In fact, they have seen thousands of living things come and go.

Why have cockroaches survived for such a long time? One reason is that they can adapt themselves to almost any environment— even the hottest, driest desert. Cockroaches are also surprisingly talented. Amazingly, they can twist their body more than twenty times a second. They can also sense even the slightest air movement. With their flat, streamlined shape and high-speed legs, they are very good at dodging and running away from their enemies. We might even call them "artful dodgers." And it is practically impossible for a cockroach to starve to death. They can eat almost anything, including other cockroaches. It is said that cockroaches could even survive a nuclear war. They can absorb at least twenty times more radiation than humans.

No.1 Is a human being the strongest living thing on earth?
No.2 What is the king of beasts?
No.3 How long have cockroaches been living on our planet?
No.4 How fast can cockroaches twist their bodies?
No.5 Why can cockroaches avoid starving to death?

Chapter 2-1
動詞の種類と文型（1）

5 文型（1）

1．第1文型（1）…主語（S）＋完全自動詞（V）
  1) **Dogs bark**.
  2) The **sun rises** in the east.
  3) **People drive** too fast on this street.
  4) **Julia** was **talk**ing with her friend.

2．第2文型（1）…主語（S）＋不完全自動詞（V）＋主格補語（SC）
  5) **He is** a **doctor**.
  6) **She is happy**.
  7) **Alice looks sad**.
  8) **She feels better** than she did this morning.

3．第3文型（1）…主語（S）＋完全他動詞（V）＋目的語（O）
  9) **I like dogs**.
  10) **They play football** every day.
  11) **You made** the same **mistakes** again.
  12) **Rachel** often **loses** her **key**.

4．第4文型（1）…主語（S）＋完全他動詞（V）＋間接目的語（IO）＋直接目的語（DO）
  13) My **uncle gave me** a **camera**. = My uncle gave a camera **to** me.
  14) **I wrote him** a long **letter**. = I wrote a long letter **to** him.
  15) **He bought me** this **bike**. = He bought this bike **for** me.
  16) **They asked her** some **questions**. = They asked some questions **of** her.

5．第5文型（1）…主語（S）＋不完全他動詞（V）＋目的語（O）＋目的格補語（OC）
  17) **We call him Ken**.
  18) **He named** his **son Taro**.
  19) **They made her happy**.
  20) **I found** this **book** very **interesting**.

Exercises

A. 次の英文の文型を述べなさい。
1. He was a teacher at this school.
2. Birds live in trees.
3. The stove keeps the room warm.
4. Mother bought me a nice present.
5. I remember her face clearly.

B. 次の英文の下線部が目的語か補語かを答えなさい。
1. George is playing the guitar.
2. She will be a nurse in the future.
3. His father is seriously ill.
4. My uncle told me an interesting story.
5. They made me happy.

C. 次の英文の下線部の語句を文末に移動させなさい。
1. Ben handed Alice the bag.
2. They asked me various questions.
3. We found the boy his key.
4. Jack will buy Jill a ring.
5. Please lend me your dictionary.

D. 次の英文を日本文に直しなさい。
1. The football season has already begun.
2. Seeing is believing.
3. You must write a letter in English.
4. I found the book very interesting.
5. She made me a Christmas cake.

E. 次の日本文を英文に直しなさい。
1. 彼らは毎年スキーをします。
2. その問題は私にはとても難しいです。
3. 私の母はあの先生をよく知っています。
4. 先生が私たちにいくつかの絵を見せてくれました。
5. 私たちは彼をキャプテンに選びました。(electを用いて)

Exercises

F. 次の英文を読み、それに続く質問に英語で答えなさい。   4

Roommates

In Japan, if you go away from home to attend college and don't live in a dormitory, you will probably live by yourself in a small apartment. Japanese students seldom have roommates. This is mainly because most apartments near universities are designed for one person only. This is not the case in many western countries like the United States and the United Kingdom. There, college students often share a large house or apartment with one or more fellow students.

Living with a roommate has several advantages. First of all, you can cut your living expenses by sharing rent and utilities costs. Second, you always have someone to talk to when you feel sad or lonely. Finally, if your roommate happens to be someone from another country, you have the opportunity to learn a new language and culture. Of course, having a roommate can also cause some problems. So before you decide to share a house or flat with someone, it is a good idea for you and your roommate to make certain rules and arrangements in advance.

Note: utilities cost：公共料金

No.1 Why don't most students in Japan live with roommates?

No.2 Where do college students often share a large house or apartment with one or more fellow students?

No.3 How can living with a roommate help cut your living expenses?

No.4 What should you do to prevent trouble with your roommate?

Chapter 2-2

動詞の種類と文型（2）

5 文型（2）

1. 第1文型（2）…主語（S）＋完全自動詞（V）
 1) **He came** to see me.
 2) **Tom grew up** in that town.
 3) There **are** some **boys** in the schoolyard.
 4) **I talked** with him on the telephone last night.

2. 第2文型（2）…主語（S）＋不完全自動詞（V）＋主格補語（SC）
 5) The **news proved false**.
 6) **It seems useless to do so**.
 7) My **aunt stays young** by doing yoga.
 8) The **writer went mad** later.

3. 第3文型（2）…主語（S）＋完全他動詞（V）＋目的語（O）
 9) **He lived** a happy **life**.
 10) **She enjoyed herself** at the party.
 11) Would **you mind opening the window**?
 12) **He wondered where she lived**.

4. 第4文型（2）…主語（S）＋完全他動詞（V）＋間接目的語（IO）＋直接目的語（DO）
 13) **She found me** a good **seat**.
 14) **I taught him how to drive**.
 15) **He told his brother where to go next**.
 16) **He asked me why she was angry**.

5. 第5文型（2）…主語（S）＋不完全他動詞（V）＋目的語（O）＋目的格補語（OC）
 17) **He heard** his **name called**.
 18) **I don't like** young **people to smoke**.
 19) **I found it of no use**.
 20) My **parents** have **made me what I am today**.

Exercises

A. 例に倣って次の英文をS、V、O、Cに分けなさい。

[例] <u>I</u> <u>am</u> very <u>happy</u>.
　　　S　V　　　　C

1. The children kept quiet for a while.
2. He told us the way to the bus stop.
3. I talked with him on the telephone last night.
4. I want you to learn English.
5. He said that he was tired.

B. 次の英文の下線部が目的語、補語、修飾語の何れであるか述べなさい。

1. I've enjoyed <u>talking</u> with you.
2. This ball is as <u>large</u> as that one.
3. We expected <u>him</u> to come soon.
4. Who is laughing so <u>loudly</u>?
5. He lived <u>to be ninety</u>.

C. 次の英文を日本文に直しなさい。

1. He always keeps early hours.
2. May I ask a favor of you?
3. The question is when he will come.
4. She will make him a good wife.
5. I found it impossible to finish the work in a day.

D. 次の日本文を英文に直しなさい。

1. 昨日は一日中雨が降りました。
2. 良い友達を選ぶことは大切なことです。
3. 彼女はなんと可愛い小鳥を飼っているのだろう。
4. 私は彼女が川に沿って歩いているのを見ました。
5. 彼は私にいつ出発すべきか教えてくれました。

Exercises

E. 次の英文を読み、それに続く質問に英語で答えなさい。 5

Take Me Out to the *Free* Ball Game

Thanks to Japanese players like Ichiro Suzuki and Hideki Matsui, Major League Baseball is nearly as popular in Japan as it is in the United States. Major League Baseball is divided into two leagues, the National League and the American League, with thirty teams altogether. Today, each team or club is made up of players of various races and nationalities. But it wasn't too long ago that racism existed even in the world of baseball in America.

During the first half of the 20th century, American baseball was segregated along racial lines. African-Americans were not allowed to play in the Major Leagues. Black baseball players were forced to play in the Negro Leagues. This racial barrier seemed impossible to overcome.

But then along came Jackie Robinson. In 1947, Jackie joined the Brooklyn Dodgers, becoming the first African-American to break this color barrier and play in the Major Leagues. But Jackie didn't have an easy time. Angry white fans often booed him. He was discriminated against in hotels and even in the locker room. But Jackie overcame these difficulties to become the National League Rookie of the Year. In 1987, the Rookie of the Year Award was officially named the Jackie Robinson Award in his honor.

Fortunately, this color barrier no longer exists. Baseball in America is now open to everyone. During each game, between the top and bottom of the seventh inning, all the fans at the ballpark, regardless of their race, nationality, and the team they are rooting for, stand up and sing "Take Me Out to the Ball Game." At this time, we can feel the ballpark become one and wonder why the color barrier ever existed.

No.1 How many leagues are there in Major League Baseball?

No.2 How many clubs are there in the Major Leagues altogether?

No.3 When were African-Americans forced to play in the Negro Leagues?

No.4 Who was the first African-American Major Leaguer?

No.5 What is the name of the song that all the spectators at a game sing together between the top and bottom of the seventh inning?

Chapter 3-1
動詞（時制）（1）

1. 現在形（1） … 現在の事実・状態、現在の習慣的動作を表す
　1) Dr. Ezaki **is** a great physicist.
　2) He usually **has** coffee at breakfast.
　3) I **know** him very well.
　4) Mother **gets** up at five every morning.
　　　※ 状態動詞 … be, know, belong, like など
　　　※ 動作動詞 … eat, visit, play, run など

2. 過去形（1） … 過去の事実・状態、過去の習慣的動作を表す
　5) It **snowed** hard last night.
　6) We **went** to the movies the day before yesterday.
　7) There **was** a big old tree on that corner in my childhood.
　8) He usually **sat** up late studying in his younger days.

3. 未来形 … 単純未来、意志未来
　9) I **shall be** twenty years old next year.
　10) It **will rain** this afternoon.
　11) She **will visit** us next month.
　12) I **am going to sell** this car.

4. 進行形（1） … 〈be動詞＋現在分詞〉
　13) He **is playing** tennis with her.
　14) They **are not studying** but **watching** TV.
　15) I **was washing** my car then.
　16) **Are** you **working** now? ― Yes, I **am**.
　　　※ 状態動詞は、原則として進行形にしない。

5. 現在完了形 … 〈have (has)＋過去分詞〉
　17) I **have** just **finished** my homework. （完了）
　18) She **has lost** her bag. （結果）
　19) He **has been** to Hawaii three times. （経験）
　20) I **have known** her for ten years. （継続）
　　　※1　I **have been studying** English for seven years.
　　　　　（過去に始まった「動作」が現在も継続中の場合）
　　　※2　It will be dark by the time I **have finished** this letter.
　　　　　（時・条件を表す副詞節の中で未来完了形の代用として）

Exercises

A. 次の英文の（　）内から適語を選びなさい。
1. There (is, are, was, were) an old temple here ten years ago.
2. My father (isn't, don't, doesn't, hasn't) drive on Sundays.
3. When did he (make, makes, made, making) the table?
4. (Will, Are, Be, Do) they go to the concert tomorrow?
5. She (belongs, is belonging, has belonged) to the tennis club for three years.

B. 次の各組の文が同じ意味になるように（　）内に適語を入れなさい。
1. { There are thirty-one days in August.
　　August (　　) thirty-one days.
2. { Dick is a hard worker.
　　Dick (　　) hard.
3. { Let's play tennis after school.
　　(　　) we play tennis after school?
4. { We are not going to visit him.
　　We (　　) visit him.
5. { It was cold yesterday and it is still cold today.
　　It has (　　) cold since yesterday.

C. 次の日本文を英文に直しなさい。
1. 彼女はどこに住んでいますか。

2. 彼はカメラを買いませんでした。

3. 誰があなたの椅子を作っているのですか。

4. 車で長崎に行くには約4時間かかるでしょう。

5. 彼女はちょうど皿を洗ったところです。

Exercises

D. 次の英文を読み、それに続く質問に英語で答えなさい。 6

Cool Biz

In the summer of 2005, the Japanese government started its Cool Biz campaign. This new policy encouraged male workers to take off their jackets and ties and to wear short-sleeved shirts while in the office. Air-conditioners were set at a comfortable 28 degrees Celsius, the temperature thought best for energy saving. Female workers were especially pleased. Before the campaign, they frequently complained about being too cold at work, since the air-conditioning was set at a temperature more suitable for men wearing coats and neckties.

By keeping the temperature at 28 degrees Celsius, the Cool Biz campaign aimed to help save energy and cut carbon dioxide emissions. Most scientists now agree that global warming is nearing a critical point, and that emissions of carbon dioxide and other greenhouse gases are a major cause of this warming trend. Let us hope that Cool Biz and other similar campaigns will make us all more aware of the danger approaching our planet.

Notes: Cool Biz campaign：クールビズキャンペーン
carbon dioxide emission：二酸化炭素の排出

No.1 When did the Japanese government start its Cool Biz campaign?

No.2 What did the Japanese government encourage workers to do?

No.3 What did female workers frequently complain about?

No.4 What do scientists say is a major cause of global warming?

Chapter 3-2

動詞（時制）(2)

1. 現在形 (2)
1) The sun **rises** in the east and **sets** in the west.（一般的な「真理・事実」）
2) He **leaves** Tokyo for Australia this evening.（確定未来）
3) He will eat dinner when Father **comes** home.（時・条件を表す副詞節で）

2. 過去形 (2)
4) I once **visited** America in my youth.（経験）
5) Care **killed** the cat.（格言などの一般的真理）

3. 進行形 (2)
6) We **are going** to Switzerland next Monday.（予定）
7) She **is** constantly **asking** me to help her.（反復）
8) He **will be studying** in France about this time next year.（未来での進行中の動作）
9) I **will be seeing** her tonight.（事の成り行き上）

4. 過去完了形 …〈had＋過去分詞〉
10) The train **had** already **started** when I arrived at the station.（完了）
11) He found that he **had left** his bag somewhere.（結果）
12) I **had** never **met** him before that.（経験）
13) We **had lived** here until then.（継続）
14) She **had been studying** abroad till last month.（継続）
15) He lost the pen which he **had bought** the day before.（大過去）

5. 未来完了形 …〈will (shall)＋have＋過去分詞〉
16) He **will have finished** studying by four.（完了）
17) He **will have gone** to Chicago by the end of this month.（結果）
18) If I go to Kirishima again, I **will have visited** it five times.（経験）
19) You **will have been** here for five years by next September.（継続）
20) She **will have been studying** abroad for two years by next month.（継続）

Exercises

A. （　　）内の動詞を適当な形に変え、下線部に書き入れなさい。

1. He _____ twenty years old next month.（be）
2. Here _____ the bus!（come）
3. She told me that she _____ London several times.（visit）
4. He _____ here for three years by next May.（live）
5. It _____ when we got off the bus.（rain）

B. 次の英文の誤りを訂正しなさい。

1. You will be poor if you will not work hard.
2. Yesterday I came across a friend of mine that I didn't see for years.
3. I don't know if he comes back tomorrow.
4. This road is leading to the city hall.
5. Matthew will be absent from school for two weeks tomorrow.

C. 下線部を過去時制に変えて、全文を書き換えなさい。

1. He <u>says</u> that the earth is round.
2. I <u>suppose</u> that she was busy.
3. I <u>hope</u> that he will win the race.
4. Tom <u>says</u> that he has never eaten cuttlefish.
5. They <u>learn</u> that Columbus discovered America.

D. 次の英文を日本文に直しなさい。

1. I was sleepy because I had been watching TV all night.
2. She was always quarreling with her brother in those days.
3. I'm sorry I have kept you waiting so long.
4. All work and no play makes Jack a dull boy.
5. I will stay here until he has finished the work.

E. 次の日本文を英文に直しなさい。

1. 彼はよく朝食前に散歩をします。
2. 君は彼から今までに何度便りをもらったことがありますか。
3. 10年後にはあなたは立派な技術者になっているでしょう。
4. 私は今晩7時には食事をしていることでしょう。（進行形で）
5. 私は彼らが入ってきたときには、もう1時間も本を読んでいました。

Exercises

F. 次の英文を読み、それに続く質問に英語で答えなさい。

Names on the Land

Place names in America reflect the country's great Native American heritage. When the Europeans arrived in North America in the 15th century, Native Americans had already been living there for nearly 25,000 years. These "Indians," as the Europeans called them, had given names to each place in their own various languages. Every mountain, river, and lake had a Native American name. European settlers kept some of these indigenous place names, and gave others new names.

About half of the state names in the United States come from Native American words. The state of Alabama was named after the Alabama, which means "thicket clearers," a tribe of farming people who cleared thickets to make space for growing food. The name Connecticut comes from a word meaning "beside the long tidal river," the tidal river in this case being the Atlantic Ocean. Massachusetts comes from a word meaning "place of a large hill," and Michigan is derived from a word that means "great water," which refers to Lake Michigan. The name Indiana isn't a Native American word, per se; it is the name given the area by European settlers and means "land of the Indians."

If you would like to know more about American place names, especially those that express its Native American heritage, try reading George R. Stewart's great book, *Names On the Land*.

No.1 When did Europeans first come to North America?

No.2 How long had Native Americans been living in North America when the Europeans arrived?

No.3 Where do about half of the state names in America come from?

No.4 What does Massachusetts mean in the original language?

No.5 What state name means "great water"?

Chapter 4-1
助動詞（1）

1. can（1）… 能力、可能、可能性、推量、許可
1) She **can** make sandwiches.
2) **Can** I use your telephone?
3) **Can** the news be true?
4) The news **cannot** be true.

2. must … 必要、義務、断定的推量
5) You **must** work harder than before.
6) He **must** be our teacher.

3. may（1）… 許可、推量、祈願
7) **May** I come in? ― Yes, you may. / Yes, please.
8) It **may** snow tonight.
9) **May** you live long!

4. will（1）… 単純・意志未来（Chapter 3 参照）、依頼
10) **Will** you open the window? ― **All right.**

5. Shall I / we ～? … 相手の意向・決断を尋ねる
11) **Shall I** turn on the radio? ― Yes, please.
12) **Shall we** go to the movies? ― Yes, let's.

6. should（1）… 義務、当然など
13) You **should** come earlier.
14) You **shouldn't** go out so late at night.

7. need … 否定文、疑問文で用いられる
15) You **needn't** buy that book.
16) **Need** I go now?

8. dare …「あえて～する」の意味で、特に、否定文、疑問文、条件文で用いられる
17) **Dare** they fight?
18) How **dare** you say such a thing?「よくもまあ～できるものだ」

9. ought to … 義務、当然、推定、期待など
19) You **oughtn't to** say such a thing.
20) That **ought to** be an exciting game.

Exercises

A. 次の英文の（　）内から適語を選びなさい。
1. She can (play, plays) the piano very well.
2. He must (be, is) sick in bed.
3. "(May, Must) I go there?" "No, you don't have to."
4. Mary (has, have) to finish the work within two hours.
5. "(Shall, Will) I help you?" "No, thank you."

B. （　）内の指示に従って書き換え、下線部に適当な語句を書き入れなさい。
1. I must leave Kagoshima.（過去の文に）
   → I ＿＿＿＿ to leave Kagoshima.
2. You can swim.（未来の文に）
   → You ＿＿＿＿ ＿＿＿＿ ＿＿＿＿ ＿＿＿＿ swim.
3. Don't open this door.（同じ意味の文に）
   → You ＿＿＿＿ open this door.
4. Please lend me your dictionary.（同じ意味の文に）
   → ＿＿＿＿ ＿＿＿＿ lend me your dictionary?
5. I will spend my holidays in Hawaii.（同じ意味の文に）
   → I ＿＿＿＿ ＿＿＿＿ ＿＿＿＿ spend my holidays in Hawaii.

C. 次の英文を日本文に直しなさい。
1. You ought not to break your word.
2. How dare you come home so late?
3. Who can that man be?

D. 次の日本文を英文に直しなさい。
1. 彼は来年何歳になりますか。
2. 明日は雨が降るかもしれません。
3. 今夜は空には何も見えません。
4. 君は約束を守るべきです。
5. 「テニスをしましょうか」「はい、しましょう」

Exercises

E. 次の英文を読み、それに続く質問に英語で答えなさい。 8

Working from Home

Custom and common sense say that employees must go to work, and must often stay late and work overtime, too. Matsushita Inc., one of Japan's largest corporations, has recently introduced a flexible new program that is changing this traditional way of doing things. The program allows most of its workers to do at least some of their work from home one or two days a week.

Such a dream-come-true system would not be possible, of course, without high-speed Internet services. Matsushita employees wishing to work from home are provided with computers and everything else they need to do their jobs. Those who benefit most from this new program are probably employees with families or elderly parents. They can do their jobs and take care of their loved ones right at home. What could be better than that?

Note: Matsushita Inc.：松下電器産業株式会社

No.1 What does Matsushita's new program allow?

No.2 How many days a week can employees work from home?

No.3 What has made this program possible?

No.4 Who gets the most benefit from this program?

Chapter 4-2
助動詞（2）

1. can（2）… 慣用表現
1) We **cannot help** admir**ing** his bravery.
2) You **cannot** study **too** hard.

2. may（2）… 譲歩、慣用表現
3) However busy he **may** be, he never fails to study English.
4) You **may well** say so.
5) You **may as well** begin at once.
6) You **might as well** throw money away **as** spend it on gambling.

3. will（2）… 主語の強い意志、習慣、傾向、推量、能力など
7) This horse **will not** move.
8) He **will** read for hours at a time.
9) Accidents **will** happen.
10) She **will** probably prove to be right.
11) This hall **will** hold three hundred people.

4. shall … 話し手の意志、聞き手の意志（疑問文で）など
12) **You shall** have that pen. = I will give you that pen.
13) **He shall** work harder. = I will have him work harder.
14) **Shall she** go there? = Do you want her to go there?

5. should（2）… 期待・可能性、また that 節で、感情・判断の原因、根拠を表す
15) She **should** arrive there by six o'clock.
16) It is **natural** that she **should** get angry.
17) They are **demand**ing that he（**should**）resign.

6. would … 過去の意志、主張、拒絶、習慣など
18) He **would not** open the door.
19) He **would often** swim there.
20) I **would rather** stay at home **than** go out.

7. used to … 過去の事実、状態、習慣など
21) There **used to** be an old church around here.
22) He **used to** keep early hours.　**Cf.** I am used to getting up early.

8. 助動詞＋完了形 … 過去の事柄に対する現在の推量、非難、後悔の気持ちを表す
23) He **may have missed** the train.
24) She **must have lost** her way.
25) Tom **cannot have said** so.
26) You **should have seen** the movie.

Exercises

A. （　）内に入る適当な助動詞を下の語群から選び、書き入れなさい。
1. He is very rude to her. She (　　) well get angry.
2. It's necessary that I (　　) wear a jacket.
3. We (　　) often play tennis in the park.
4. There (　　) to be an elementary school over there.
   [can, may, should, used, would]

B. 次の英文の（　）内から適語を選びなさい。
1. Dogs (will, shall) bark at strangers.
2. I (should, would) say she's over fifty.
3. She (would, used to) love him, but now she doesn't.
4. She is not honest. She (cannot, must) have stolen the key.

C. 次の各組の文が同じ意味になるように（　）内に適語を入れなさい。
1. { It is impossible that he has come back so early.
    He (　　) (　　) (　　) back so early.
2. { You shall hear from me.
    I (　　) write to you.
3. { I am sorry that you didn't see the film.
    You (　　) (　　) seen the film.
4. { He insisted on my going there.
    He insisted that I (　　) (　　) there.

D. 次の日本文を英文に直しなさい。
1. 彼は私の言うことに耳を傾けようとしません。(willを用いて)

2. 君は彼を訪ねる必要はなかったのに。(needを用いて)

3. この電車は10時までには博多に着くはずです。(shouldを用いて)

Exercises

E. 次の英文を読み、それに続く質問に英語で答えなさい。

Hawai'i, Hawaii, and the Aloha Spirit

Hawaii is now one of the most popular tourist resorts in the world. Every day, thousands of visitors flock to this tiny island paradise in the center of the Pacific Ocean. And each and every visitor is welcomed with the Aloha Spirit, the islands' spirit of friendship and hospitality.

Aloha is a native Hawaiian word meaning love. It is used as both greeting and farewell, and signifies the sentiments of affection, kindness, sympathy, and love. Aloha also represents Hawaiians' love of life and art of living. To native Hawaiians, wealth has never meant the accumulation of many things and possessions. To Hawaiians, wealth is simply the joy of sharing and giving.

Like the indigenous peoples of North America, Australia, and Hokkaido, native Hawaiians had their land taken away from them. Their unique culture and way of thinking were all but destroyed by invading outsiders.

Hawaii became a U.S. territory in 1898. In 1959, it became the fiftieth state in the Union. Since then, development has turned the islands into one big tourist resort. Waikiki Beach is a prime example of what has happened to the islands. Before it became a major tourist mecca, Waikiki was a field of taro, a staple of the native Hawaiian diet. Now, many native Hawaiians are asserting their rights as the islands' true owners. Is it any wonder?

Today, we often come across the word "Hawai'i" when we visit the islands. This spelling, say native Hawaiians, better reflects the native pronunciation of the word. By spelling it this way, they stress their claim that the land was originally theirs. To native Hawaiians, Hawaii will always be Hawai'i.

No.1 What does Aloha mean?
No.2 Were there indigenous people in Japan?
No.3 When did Hawaii become an American territory?
No.4 What is a staple of the native Hawaiian diet?
No.5 Why is Hawaii intentionally spelled Hawai'i by native Hawaiians?

Chapter 5-1
能動態と受動態（1）

1. S＋V＋Oの文
1) Everybody **respects** Tom. → Tom **is respected by** everybody.
2) He **washed** the car. → The car **was washed by** him.
3) They **speak** English in America. → English **is spoken**（**by them**）in America.

2. S＋V＋O＋Oの文
4) She **teaches us** English. → We **are taught English by** her.
　　　　　　　　　　　　　　→ English **is taught to us by** her.
5) Her mother **bought her** a doll. → A doll **was bought for her by** her mother.
　　※ 動詞が**buy**や**make**などの場合は、ふつう間接目的語を主語にした受動態にはしない。
6) I **asked him** a trivial question. → He **was asked** a trivial question **by** me.
　　　　　　　　　　　　　　　　　　→ A trivial question **was asked of him by** me.

3. S＋V＋O＋Cの文
7) They **elected** him **mayor**. → He **was elected mayor**（by them）.
8) I **found** the book **interesting**. → The book **was found interesting by** me.
9) We **call** the dog "**Shiro**." → The dog **is called** "Shiro"（by us）.
　　※ 補語（C）は、受動態の主語にはなれない。

4. 助動詞のある文
10) I **must do** the work today. → The work **must be done**（by me）today.
11) We **can see** that mountain. → That mountain **can be seen**（by us）.
12) You **should study** English harder. → English **should be studied** harder（by you）.

5. 受動態の否定文と疑問文
13) They **don't sell** books at the store. → Books **aren't sold** at the store.
14) Do they **sell** books at the store? → **Are** books **sold** at the store?
15) She **didn't invite** them to the party. → They **weren't invited** to the party by her.
16) **Did** she **invite** them to the party? → **Were** they **invited** to the party by her?
17) **Nobody thanked** me. → I **was not thanked by anybody**.

6. 動作と状態（be動詞以外の動詞を使って区別することもある。）
18) The store **was closed** at 8 p.m.（動作）
19) The store **is closed** every Monday.（状態）
20) Ted **got hurt** in a traffic accident.（動作）
21) They **lay hidden** in the bushes.（状態）

Exercises

A. 次の英文を受動態に書き換えなさい。
1. Everybody loves his mother.
2. She read the book.
3. He taught them Chinese.
4. She cooked me some sausages.
5. We painted the door green.

B. 次の英文の（ ）内から適当な語句を選びなさい。
1. I was sent to school by (he, his, him).
2. She is (pleased, pleasing, pleased with) her new dress.
3. The tree was (cut, cutting, cuts) down by John.
4. (Did, Was, Had) the top of the mountain covered with snow?
5. (Are you interested, Are you interest, Do you interest) in Japanese history?

C. 次の英文の（ ）内から適語を選びなさい。
1. Butter is made (by, into, from) milk.
2. The chair is made (of, by, from) wood.
3. Milk is made (of, into, by) cheese.
4. The desks are made (into, from, by) them.
5. The car is made (at, in, by) Japan.

D. 次の日本文を受動態の英文に直しなさい。
1. この犬小屋は彼が作りました。

2. この古い車は今は使われていません。

3. この歌は若い人たちによく歌われています。

4. 彼女はそのプレゼントに満足しています。

5. そのバケツ (bucket) には水がいっぱい入っています。

Exercises

E. 次の英文を読み、それに続く質問に英語で答えなさい。 10

Football

Most people know that many sports— cricket, rugby, football— originated in England. But among these, football is far and away the most popular. It started out as a violent game played by young people in the mean streets of London. By the mid-19th century, football had grown into a true sport with a sophisticated set of rules, and had become a central part of life for the British working classes.

As the British Empire grew, more and more Britons began working abroad, and they took football along with them. Before long, the sport was being played all over the globe. Although football is now an international sport— perhaps the most popular in the world— England is still recognized as its birthplace. That's why the English Premier League is so internationally respected. The leading teams in the League, such as Liverpool and Arsenal, have some of the world's top players on their rosters. David Beckham, for example, used to play for one of the League's top teams, Manchester United. Today, he makes a huge salary and is treated like a Hollywood star. In fact, he now lives in Hollywood.

Note: sophisticated：精巧な、複雑な

No.1 What was football like before it grew into a true sport?

No.2 For whom did football become a central part of life?

No.3 What is the name of the internationally respected professional football league in England?

No.4 Which English team did David Beckham used to play for?

Chapter 5-2

能動態と受動態（2）

1. 完了形、進行形の場合
 A. 完了形の文 … **have**（**has, had, will have**）＋**been**＋過去分詞
 1) She **has bought** the doll. → The doll **has been bought by** her.
 2) He **had finished** the task by ten. → The task **had been finished by** him by ten.
 B. 進行形の文
 3) They **were singing** the song. → The song **was being sung by** them.

2. 疑問詞を用いた疑問文の場合
 4) **Where did** you **buy** it? → **Where was** it **bought by** you?
 5) **Who discovered** America? → **By whom was** America **discovered**?
  → **Who was** America **discovered by**?（口語）

3. 「自動詞＋前置詞」が他動詞の働きをしている場合
 6) His friends **laughed at** him. → He **was laughed at by** his friends.
 7) She **took good care of** the sick. → The sick **were taken good care of by** her.
  → **Good care was taken of** the sick **by** her.

4. 命令文の場合 … Let＋目的語＋be＋過去分詞
 8) **Bring some water**. → **Let some water be brought**.

5. 目的語が節である場合
 9) **They say that** he **is** a doctor. → **It is said that** he is a doctor.
  → He **is said to be** a doctor.
 10) **They believe that** she worked there. → **It is believed that** she worked there.
  → She **is believed to have worked** there.

6. 知覚・使役動詞の場合
 11) Jane **saw** him **cross** the street. → He **was seen to cross** the street by Jane.
 12) He **made** her **go** there. → She **was made to go** there by him.
  Cf. He had his someone steal wallet. → He had his wallet stolen.

7. by 以外の前置詞を使う受動態
 13) Everybody in the village **knows** him. → He is **known to** everybody in the village.
 14) The sight **surprised** her. → She **was surprised at** the sight.
 15) The game **absorbed** the children. → The children **were absorbed in** the game.
 16) The news **pleased** us. → We **were pleased with**［at］the news.
  ※ 驚く、喜ぶなどの感情を表す場合、英語では受動態を用いるが、日本語では「～される」と訳さない方がより自然である。

Exercises

A. 次の英文の（　）内から適当な語句を選びなさい。

1. The house was felt (shake, to shake, shook) by me.
2. Not a soul can (see, be seeing, be seen) on the street.
3. By whom (was he brought, did he bring, he was brought) up?

B. 日本文と同じ意味になるように、（　）内に適語を入れなさい。

1. 私は通りで知らない人に話しかけられました。
   I was (　) (　) (　) a stranger in the street.
2. この魚は英語で何と呼ばれますか。
   (　) (　) this fish (　) in English?
3. 彼女の父は医者だったそうです。
   (　) (　) (　) that her father was a doctor.

C. 次の英文の態を換えなさい。

1. You must take good care of the baby. →
2. A truck ran over the dog. →
3. Everyone thinks that he is a great scholar. →

D. 次の各組の英文を、意味の違いに注意して日本文に直しなさい。

1.
   a. His car was washed by him.
   b. He had his car washed.

2.
   a. The gates get closed at five p.m.
   b. The gates are closed today.

3.
   a. He is known to all his villagers.
   b. A person is known by the company he keeps.

E. 次の日本文を英文に直しなさい。

1. 彼らはそのサッカーの試合に興奮しました。

2. 私は母に散髪をしてもらいました。

3. 彼はただで働かされました。

Exercises

F. 次の英文を読み、それに続く質問に英語で答えなさい。

Wedding Anniversaries and Family Harmony

The practice of giving gifts on wedding anniversaries started in Germany. Friends gave a wreath of silver to a wife who had lived with her husband for 25 years. Silver symbolized the harmony that is essential to any marriage. A woman who had been married 50 years received a wreath of gold. This is how the 25th and 50th anniversaries became known as the silver wedding anniversary and golden wedding anniversary, respectively.

While this gift-giving idea came from Germany, the custom of actually celebrating wedding anniversaries probably originated in Britain. In the beginning, only five anniversaries were celebrated: the fifth, fifteenth, twentieth, fiftieth, and sixtieth. But when the custom was introduced to America, many other wedding anniversaries were added and celebrated with special symbolic gifts. Paper represented one year of marriage, cotton or straw two years, silk or linen twelve years, pearls 30 years, and diamonds 75 years.

In Japan, tradition held that the bond between the two families was more important than that between the husband and wife, so wedding anniversaries were not customarily celebrated. Not until 1894, that is. That's when, or so the story goes, Japan's first wedding anniversary— the silver anniversary of the Emperor Meiji— was celebrated. The custom has been popular ever since.

Japan now has fifteen official holidays, days set aside each year to celebrate important events, people, and ideas. Perhaps every family should make its wedding anniversary a sort of sixteenth official holiday— an annual event to strengthen family ties and promote family harmony.

No.1 Where did the practice of giving gifts on wedding anniversaries start?

No.2 How many kinds of wedding anniversaries were there in the UK in the beginning?

No.3 Why weren't wedding anniversaries popular among the Japanese?

No.4 When was the first celebration of a wedding anniversary held in Japan?

No.5 Who celebrated a wedding anniversary first in Japan?

Chapter 6-1

名詞（1）

1. 普通名詞 … 数えられて、複数形あり
   1) I have a **book** in my **hand**.
   2) I am a **student**, and they are **students**, too.
   3) Many **cars** are running along the **street**.

2. 集合名詞 … 数えられて、複数形あり
   4) My **family is** very large.（集合体として）
   5) My **family are all** early risers.（構成員に着目）
   6) There **are** ten **families** in the apartment house.
      ※ 他に、class, crew, people, team, etc.

3. 物質名詞 … 単数形のみで、数える場合は容器や量の単位などを併用
   7) Please give me **a glass of water**.
   8) There is **a little wine** in this bottle.
      ※ 他に、a bottle of beer, a cup of tea, a cake of soap, a loaf of bread, a sheet of paper, a slice of ham, a spoonful of sugar, etc.

4. 抽象名詞 … 単数形のみ
   9) **Honesty** is the best policy.
   10) Everyone seeks **happiness**.

5. 固有名詞 … 大文字で書き始める
   11) **George Washington** was the first president of the United States.
   12) **Mt. Fuji** is the highest mountain in Japan.
   13) **The Tanakas** like cats and dogs.
      ※ the ＋姓の複数形 …「～夫妻、～家の人々」

6. 名詞の性
   14) 男性 **boy, brother, king, actor**, etc.　　… **he, they**
   15) 女性 **girl, sister, queen, actress**, etc.　… **she, they**
   16) 通性 **child, parent, friend, student**, etc. … **he** or **she, they**
   17) 中性 **door, river, book, ship**, etc.　　　… **it, they**

7. 名詞の複数形
   18) 規則的（＊は例外）: **cow -- cows, boy -- boys, bus -- buses, box -- boxes, fly -- flies, potato -- potatoes,** *****piano -- pianos, calf -- calves, *****roof -- roofs**
   19) 不規則的: **foot -- feet, woman -- women, mouse -- mice, ox -- oxen, deer - deer, Chinese -- Chinese, brother-in-law -- brothers-in-law, passerby -- passersby**
   20) その他: **a pair of glasses** (**scissors, shoes, trousers**), **mathematics, physics**

Exercises

A. （　）内の語を正しい形にして下線部に書きなさい。
1. There are some _____ on the desk. (pencil)
2. Mr. White has three _____. (daughter)
3. How many _____ do you have? (child)
4. Our grandfather told us a lot of interesting _____. (story)

B. （　）内に入る適語を下の語群から選び、正しい形にして書き入れなさい。
1. My brother drank two (　　) of hot coffee this morning.
2. Bring me a (　　) of red chalk, please.
3. Please put a (　　) of sugar in my tea.
4. I bought two (　　) of bread yesterday.
   〔glass, cup, loaf, piece, lump〕

C. 次の各文の下線部の名詞を複数形にして文全体を書き換えなさい。
1. A girl plays with her toy. →
2. That looker-on is a Japanese. →
3. An ox doesn't give us milk. →
4. There was a goose in the pond. →

D. 次の各文の（　）内に、文中にある名詞と反対の性を表す語を入れなさい。
1. Many (　　) and gentlemen were dancing to the music.
2. I have two (　　) and three nieces.
3. The farmer keeps several roosters and many (　　).
4. The (　　) works in the garden and his wife cooks in the kitchen.

E. 次の日本文を英文に直しなさい。
1. どうか私に水を一杯ください。

2. 兄は新しい靴を一足買いました。

3. あなたのクラスには何人の学生がいますか。

4. 部屋には古いテーブルが一つありました。

Exercises

F. 次の英文を読み、それに続く質問に英語で答えなさい。

Japanese Food

    A standard Japanese meal consists of a bowl of cooked rice, some miso soup, and several different "side" dishes made from vegetables, meat, fish, and tofu. This type of meal, because it is highly nutritious as well as low in fat and calories, has been attracting a lot of attention lately.

    However, it is not necessarily true that the average Japanese person eats this standard meal three times a day. A traditional Japanese breakfast consists of rice, miso soup, and one other dish (such as grilled fish), with green tea. But many people today favor a western-style breakfast, with toast, bacon and eggs, and coffee. At lunch, many Japanese choose noodles, which originated in China, or pasta as an alternative to the rice-based meal.

    While dinner is considered to be the most important meal of the day, it is not always the traditional, standard one. For their evening meal, many Japanese enjoy a variety of cuisines from all around the world, though many dishes have been altered somewhat to better fit the Japanese palate.

Notes: cuisine：料理（法）　palate：味覚

No.1 Why are Japanese meals attracting attention?

No.2 What does a traditional Japanese breakfast consist of?

No.3 What do some Japanese people sometimes eat at lunch instead of a rice-based meal?

No.4 Why are many foreign dishes altered?

Chapter 6-2 名詞（2）

1. 注意すべき名詞
1) He threw **a stone** at the dog.（物質）→（普通）
2) She was **a beauty** when she was young.（抽象）→（普通）
3) He is **a Newton**.（固有）→（普通）

2. 文中での働き
4) 主格、所有格、目的格
   The **book** on the desk is mine. / He is a famous **writer**.（主格）
   Tom's uncle lives in this town.（所有格）
   I know the **principal** of your school.（目的格）
5) 所有格の作り方
   ① 生物を表す語 … **-'s**（但し、**s**で終わる複数形 **-s'**）
      the **boy's** box, a **girls'** school
      My **father's** office is in the center of the city.
   ② 無生物を表す語 … **of** を用いる
      the top **of Mt. Fuji**, the lid **of the bottle**
      We can see the red roof **of his house** over there.
      ※ 但し、次のような場合には **-'s**（**-s'**）をつける
         the **earth's** surface（擬人化）
         today's paper, fifty **miles'** distance（時間、金額、距離、重量を表す語）
         at one's **wits'**［**wit's**］end「途方にくれて」（慣用句）
   ③ **this**, **that**, **some** などの語との併用（語順に注意）
      that dog of my **uncle's**, **some** books of **Ben's**

3. 注意すべき複数形
6) 外来語の複数形
   bacterium → bacteria,   **datum → data**,
   oasis → oases,   **basis → bases**
7) 文字、数字、記号の複数形は原則として **-'s** をつける
   PTA's,   **5's**,   **four H's**
8) 複数形で特別な意味になる名詞
   good（善）→ **goods**（商品），   **spectacle**（光景）→ **spectacles**（眼鏡）
   arm（腕）→ **arms**（武器），   **custom**（習慣）→ **customs**（関税）

Exercises

A. 次の英文の（ ）内から適語を選びなさい。
1. The Japanese (is, are) said to be an industrious people.
2. This bridge is made of (stone, stones).
3. Mathematics (is, are) my favorite subject.
4. My sister takes a monthly (lady's, ladies') magazine.
5. The committee (is, are) divided in their opinions.

B. 次の文の誤りを正しなさい。
1. The room's door is open.
2. More than a hundred peoples were injured.
3. A few minute's walk brought us to the station.
4. This my father's car is not running.
5. I am going to stay at my aunt for a week.

C. 次の英文を日本文に直しなさい。
1. I have a few pennies with me.
2. What do the three R's mean?
3. We should read the lives of great men and women.
4. He is a famous man of letters.
5. A Mr. Smith came to see you during your absence.

D. 次の日本文を英文に直しなさい。
1. 私のカメラはコダック (Kodak) です。
2. ジャックのこのラケットは新しいですね。
3. 良夫君のお母さんは女子高校の先生です。
4. 私は理髪店で彼に会いました。

Exercises

E. 次の英文を読み、それに続く質問に英語で答えなさい。

No Red Pandas, Please

It is no exaggeration to say that the giant panda is the most popular "idol" in the animal world. Its endearing looks and charming movements never fail to cheer us up and bring a smile to our faces. We can see these beautiful animals in many zoos around the globe. But the forests of China where they live in the wild are disappearing, and so are the pandas themselves. Biologists, environmentalists, and animal rights activists are working round the clock to protect the panda and its natural habitat.

The International Union for the Conservation of Nature and Natural Resources (IUCN) recently entered the giant panda in its Red Data Book. This is a collection of data on plants and animals that are "turning red," that is, that are in danger of extinction. Some scientists estimate that more than 40 animal and plant species are dying out every year.

There are five factors that can contribute to a species' becoming endangered: habitat destruction, excessive harvesting, the introduction of alien species, air and water pollution, and natural disasters. The first four factors are man-made. In other words, they are preventable.

What we need to do first of all is to fully grasp the present state of the environment. We need to be fully aware of how bad things really are. Then we must do everything we can to keep animal habitats from being destroyed further. We must make every effort to keep our beloved black-and-white pandas from turning red.

No.1 What is happening to the giant pandas in China?
No.2 Who is working hard to protect giant pandas?
No.3 What kind of book is the Red Data Book?
No.4 About how many species die out every year?
No.5 What four factors that can contribute to a species' becoming endangered are man-made?

Chapter 7-1
冠詞と数詞（1）

1. 不定冠詞（a, an）の用法（1）

1) She waited for **an** hour. （「ひとつの」）
2) **A** cat can see in the dark. （総称的）
    = **The cat** can see in the dark.
    = **Cats** can see in the dark.
3) I work about eight hours **a** [= **per**] day.

2. 定冠詞（the）の用法（1）

4) There is a book there. **The** book is written in English. （前述の名詞の指示）
5) Shut **the** door. （周囲の状況、前後関係から自明なもの）
6) **The** earth moves around **the** sun. （唯一のもの）
7) Mt. Fuji is **the** highest mountain in Japan. （最上級や序数の前）
8) He likes playing **the guitar**. （楽器名）
    Cf. They are playing **soccer**. （競技名）

3. 冠詞の省略（1）

9) **Mother** has gone shopping. （肉親を表す語）
10) I have **breakfast** at seven. （食事名）
    Cf. She had **a nice dinner** yesterday. （修飾語付き）
11) We walked to **school**. （授業）
    Cf. We walked to **the school**. （建物）
12) **by bus**, **on foot**, **at night** （慣用句）

4. 数詞（1）

13) 基数詞と（序数詞）

    one(first), **two**(second), **three**(third), **four**(fourth), **five**(fifth),
    nine(ninth), **twenty**(twentieth), **forty-two**(forty-second),
    hundred(hundredth)

14) 数字の読み方（1）

    ① 整数
    2,106,538 : **two million, one hundred（and）six thousand, five hundred（and）thirty-eight**

    ② 年号、月日
    1985 : **nineteen eighty-five**；1900 **nineteen hundred**
    10月6日 : **October（the）sixth / the sixth of October**

    ③ 時刻
    1時10分 : **ten past one / one ten**；1時半 : **half past one / one thirty**；
    1時45分 : **a quarter to two / one forty-five**

    ④ 電話番号
    092-938-2659 : **oh nine two / nine three eight / two six five nine**

Exercises

A. 次の文の（ ）内に適当な冠詞を入れなさい。不要な箇所には×印をつけなさい。
1. I have (   ) dinner in (   ) evening.
2. What (   ) interesting book this is!
3. He told his assistant to close (   ) window.
4. He plays (   ) tennis and she plays (   ) violin after school.
5. By (   ) way, who opened (   ) drawers?

B. 次の数字を英語で読みなさい。
1. 34,512
2. 1963年8月7日
3. 昭和20年
4. 862－3075（電話番号）
5. 10時15分
6. 6時50分

C. 次の英文を日本文に直しなさい。
1. A black and white dog is lying there.

2. That clock loses five seconds a day.

3. The boy was in a hurry.

4. If the weather is fine, I'll go for a walk.

5. Look at the yellow bird on the roof.

D. 次の日本文を英文に直しなさい。
1. 人々はふつう飛行機でそこへ行きます。

2. 彼は週に2回泳ぎに行きます。

3. その電車はまもなく博多駅に着きます。

4. 私は彼に英和辞典を買ってあげた。

5. ローマは一日にして成らず。

Exercises

E. 次の英文を読み、それに続く質問に英語で答えなさい。

Please Don't Talk and Drive

Do you know anyone who doesn't have a mobile phone? Probably not. Over the past ten years the mobile phone has gone from novelty item to absolute necessity. Mobiles have made keeping in touch with friends and family quick and easy. They have improved our lives in all sorts of ways. But the mobile phone is not without serious problems. Of these, talking while driving is the most serious of all. Drivers who chat on their phones while behind the wheel are causing more and more traffic accidents. Some drivers even read and send text messages! Could anything be more dangerous?

Many countries have already passed laws that restrict the use of mobile phones by drivers. Most ban the use of handheld phones, but permit the use of hand-free phones. Japan, on the other hand, prohibits both. Is Japan too strict? Absolutely not! Studies show that most mobile-related traffic accidents occur when drivers talk and drive. It doesn't seem to make any difference whether the conversation takes place on a handheld or hand-free phone. This suggests that it is the conversation itself that is the main cause of traffic accidents.

Notes: handheld：手で持った（状態の）　hand-free：手を放した（状態の）

No.1 What is the mobile phone these days?

No.2 What are drivers who talk while driving causing?

No.3 What country bans drivers from using both handheld and hand-free mobiles?

No.4 Is using hand-free mobiles while driving safer than using handheld mobiles?

Chapter 7-2
冠詞と数詞 (2)

1. 不定冠詞の用法 (2)
1) She has **a** knowledge of politics. 「ある程度の」
2) He wants to be **an** Edison. 「～という人、～のような人」
3) I have **a** Ford. 「～の作品、～の製品」

2. 定冠詞の用法 (2)
4) He seized her by **the** arm. （人体の一部分を指して）
5) My grade in English was in **the** eighties. （-tiesで終わる複数形と共に）
6) **The rich** are not always happy. (the rich = rich people)
   They pursued **the beautiful**. (the beautiful = beauty)
7) We hired a boat by **the** hour. （単位を示す）
8) **the** Nile, **the** Pacific Ocean, **the** New Tokaido Line, **the** Mainichi, **the** White House, **the** Alps, **the** Philippines （河川、海洋、列車路線、新聞・雑誌、公共建造物、山脈、群島などの名称に）例外：Tokyo Bay, Lake Biwa

3. 冠詞の省略 (2)
9) **Little boy**, where are you going? （呼びかけ語）
10) Mr. Wood, **president** of the firm, invited me to the party. （補語や同格として用いられた身分・官職・公職を表す語）
11) **Summer** comes after **spring**. （季節名）
    Cf. The accident happened in **the winter of 2006**.
12) **from beginning to end**, **hand in hand**, **take plac**e など（慣用句）

4. 数詞 (2)
13) 数字の読み方 (2)
    ① 小数、分数
    25.106 : twenty-five point one zero six
    $\frac{1}{2}$: a half, $\frac{1}{4}$: a quarter, $\frac{2}{5}$: two fifths, $2\frac{7}{8}$: two and seven eighths
    ② その他
    Elizabeth Ⅱ　Elizabeth **the Second**
    World War Ⅱ　World War **Two** or the **Second** World War
14) 加減乗除
    $2 + 3 = 5$: **Two** plus **three** equals **five**.
    $5 - 2 = 3$: **Five** minus **two** equals **three**.
    $2 \times 3 = 6$: **Two** times **three** equals **six**.
    $6 \div 2 = 3$: **Six** divided by **two** equals **three**.

Exercises

A. 次の文の（ ）内に適当な冠詞を入れなさい。不要な箇所には×印をつけなさい。
1. They are nearly of (　　) age.
2. As it is (　　) fine weather, let's go on (　　) picnic.
3. Pencils are sold by (　　) dozen.
4. (　　) hero as he was, he was assassinated.

B. 次の各文の（ ）内の語を正しく並べなさい。
1. She is (cook, a, so, good).
2. (houses, the, all) were destroyed by the fire.
3. (a, of, all, sudden), the old man fell down.
4. I am (stranger, quite, a) here.

C. 次の英文を日本文に直しなさい。
1. The child is father of the man.

2. He saw a church at a distance.

3. They live from hand to mouth.

4. She stared me in the face.

5. He says that the poor are the oppressed.

D. 次の日本文を英文に直しなさい。
1. 私はこんな美しい庭園を見たことがありません。

2. 彼女たちは週給で働いています。

3. 父は商用で7時半発の特急で上京しました。

4. 紳士というものは、いつも他人に親切です。

Exercises

E. 次の英文を読み、それに続く質問に英語で答えなさい。

Money Talks

As an old saying goes, money talks. In other words, money decides just about everything. It makes almost anything possible. But money also "talks" in a more literal sense. It tells us a lot about history, culture, and so on.

The currency of the United States of America consists of dollars and cents. The Europeans who settled North America brought their home countries' bills and coins with them. These were used in trade and business until 1775, when the American colonies started making their own money. In that year, the first dollars, made of paper, were issued. Silver dollars appeared in 1794.

Today, there are seven different bill denominations and six different coins. Each coin has a nickname. Americans call a one-cent coin a penny. A five-cent coin is a nickel, a ten-cent coin a dime, and a twenty-five cent coin is known as a quarter. Each coin is stamped with a portrait of a historical figure, including Abraham Lincoln, Thomas Jefferson, Franklin Roosevelt, and George Washington. All the bill denominations feature portraits of famous Americans as well. Many people call U.S. dollars "greenbacks." This name goes back to the American Civil War, when Abraham Lincoln was president. The Secretary of the Treasury decided that the back of each bill should be printed in green on a white background— hence, greenback.

Not too long ago, the United States issued fifty new quarters, each with a special design representing a different state of the Union. Now, lots of Americans have started collecting these quarters. Why don't you try collecting all fifty, too? You don't have to be rich to enjoy listening to these new coins "talk" about the fifty American states.

No.1 Who first brought coins and paper money to America?

No.2 When were the first paper dollars issued in America?

No.3 When did the first silver dollars appear?

No.4 How many bill denominations are there in America?

No.5 Why are dollars called greenbacks?

Chapter 8-1

代名詞（1）

1. **人称代名詞（1）** … 1人称・2人称・3人称、単数・複数、主格・所有格・目的格の区別がある：1人称単数（**I, my, me**）、2人称単数（**you, your, you**）、3人称単数（**he, his, him; she, her, her; it, its, it**）、1人称複数（**we, our, us**）、2人称複数（**you, your, you**）、3人称複数（**they, their, them**）

   1) Do **you** know **her** sister?
   2) **I** saw **them** yesterday.

2. **所有代名詞「〜のもの」**：単数（**mine, yours, his, hers**）、複数（**ours, yours, theirs**）

   3) Is that house **yours** or **theirs**?
   4) She is a friend of **mine**.

3. **再帰代名詞（1）**：単数（**myself, yourself, himself, herself, itself**）、複数（**ourselves, yourselves, themselves**）

   5) I enjoyed **myself** at the party.（再帰用法）
   6) He **himself** did it.（同格的に用いて強調する）
   7) She made the bookcase **by herself**.（慣用句）

4. **疑問代名詞**

   8) **Which** do you like better, this or that?
   9) **What** do you call your dog?
   10) **Whose** is this bicycle?
   11) I don't know **who** she is.（間接疑問文）

5. **指示代名詞（1）**

   12) **That** is Alice's brother.
   13) **These** are my children.
       Cf. Are **those cats** yours?（指示形容詞）

6. **不定代名詞（1）**

   14) **All** of the students **are** absent.　*Cf.* **All is** well with her.
   15) This car is mine. That **one** is my wife's.
   16) I have two sons. **One** is in Fukuoka, and **the other** is in Kyoto.
   17) **Both** of them can speak French.
   18) He didn't say **anything**.
   19) **Each** of the students has a car.

7. **It の特別用法（1）**

   20) How far is **it** from here to the station?（距離）
   21) What time is **it**?（時刻）
   22) **It** is getting dark.（明暗）
   23) **It** is hard **to get up early in winter**.（仮主語で to get... を指す）

Exercises

A. 次の英文の（　）内から適語を選びなさい。
1. I don't want this motorcycle. Do you want (it, one)?
2. Do you know (that, those) girls?
3. "(Who, Whose) book is this?" "It's my brother's."
4. He said to (his, himself), "What's the matter with her?"
5. I have two pens. One is long and (another, the other) is short.
6. (Each, Every) of the girls has her own camera.
7. I have no bag. I want (one, it).
8. (What, Which) of the books do you want to take?
9. "(Who, What) is she?" "She is a nurse."
10. (Either, Both) you or I must go there.

B. （　）内の語を正しい形にして下線部に書き入れなさい。
1. She visited _____ the day before yesterday. (he)
2. Is that bicycle _____ or his? (she)
3. Both of _____ are alive. (they)
4. Do you know _____ bicycle that is? (who)
5. I bowed to him and seated _____ . (I)

C. 次の日本文を英文に直しなさい。
1. 明日は晴れるでしょう。

2. 今日は何曜日ですか。

3. あなたの家からその図書館までどのくらい距離がありますか。

4. 車でそこへ行くのにどのくらい時間がかかりますか。

5. 早起きすることは良いことです。

Exercises

D. 次の英文を読み、それに続く質問に英語で答えなさい。

The Female vs. Male Brain

For a long time, people (mostly men) assumed that males were intellectually superior to females because their brains were bigger. Some research has shown that a boy's brain is already 12-20 percent larger at birth than a girl's. But does this mean that boys are naturally smarter? No, it doesn't. The connection between brain size and intellectual competence has never been proven.

Some scientists have tried to show that behavioral differences between men and women have something to do with differences in the way their brains function. For instance, women are often said to have superior verbal, that is, language abilities, while men are better at processing spatial information. Interestingly, one study found that women in love display more activity in the area of the brain that governs memory than men in love do. At any rate, it seems as if we have a long way to go before we can understand how the brain, female or male, actually works.

Notes: competence：能力　function：働く

No.1 Why did some people assume that men were intellectually superior to women?

No.2 What has never been proven?

No.3 In what abilities are women said to be superior to men?

No.4 In what area of the brain do women show more activity than men when they fall in love?

Chapter 8-2
代名詞（2）

1. 人称代名詞（2）…「一般の人々」を表す we, you, they
1) **We** should love **our** neighbors.
2) **You** cannot tell what will happen tomorrow.
3) **They** speak English in this country.

2. 指示代名詞（2）
4) **The ears** of a cat are shorter than **those** of a rabbit.（名詞の反復を避けるため）
5) God helps **those** who help themselves.（「人々」）
6) He said that **he had been sick in bed**, but **that** was not true.（前述の内容を表す）
7) The boys said **this**: **a red car hit the man and drove away**.（後述の内容を表す）
8) There is a bicycle beside the blue car; **this** [= **the car**] is my father's and **that** [= **the bicycle**] is mine.（後者、前者）
9) Do it yourself, **and that** at once.（「しかも」の意）
10) He is a gentleman, and ought to be treated **as such**.（「そのようなものとして」の意）

3. 再帰代名詞（2）
11) Help **yourself** to the wine.（再帰用法）
12) She is beauty **itself**.（同格的に用いて強調する）
　= She is very beautiful.
13) She was **beside herself** with joy.（慣用句）

4. 不定代名詞（2）
14) I will give you **either** of the two books.
15) **Neither** of my parents is dead.
16) **One** should always keep **one's** word.（漠然と人を表す）
17) **None** of them were present.
18) I don't like this hat. Show me **another**.

5. It の特別用法（2）
19) **It** is all over now.「万事休す」（状況）
20) **It** is kind of you **to show me the way**.（仮主語）
21) **It** is no use **crying over spilt milk**.（仮主語）
22) **It** is doubtful **whether he will come or not**.（仮主語）
23) I think **it** natural **for you to say so**.（仮目的語）
24) What **was it that** Dick broke?（強調構文）

Exercises

A. 次の英文の（　）内から適語を選びなさい。

1. (All, Everyone) should keep his or her promises.
2. There was no objection on the part of (these, those) present.
3. Please make (you, yourself) at home.
4. They accepted the offer, and (this, that) with thanks.
5. "Have a nice summer vacation." "(Such, The same) to you."

B. 次の文の（　）内に適当な代名詞を入れなさい。

1. When (　) comes to jazz, she's an expert.
2. Be kind to (　) who are around you.
3. To say is one thing, and to do is quite (　).
4. (　) seemed that he had been rich.
5. The heavy rain made (　) impossible for us to go there.

C. 次の英文を日本文に直しなさい。

1. He was patience itself.
2. She came to herself soon after the accident.
3. After that I occupied myself in writing to them.
4. He thinks he is somebody.
5. Any of you can participate in the contest.

D. 次の日本文を英文に直しなさい。

1. ベンが昨日買ったのはこの本でした。
2. この少年たちは誰もその事実を知りません。
3. 大学へ行く人もいれば行かない人もいます。
4. 彼は数学ではクラスの誰にも劣りません。(second to none を用いて)
5. まもなく梅雨に入るでしょう。(It を用いて)

Exercises

E. 次の英文を読み、それに続く質問に英語で答えなさい。

We All Scream for Ice Cream

It is safe to say that ice cream is the world's favorite dessert. But it is not so easy to say just when this cool and refreshing confection was created. One thing for sure, it did not happen overnight. The development of ice cream was a long, historical process.

Tradition has it that it was the Chinese who invented ice cream some two thousand years ago. But it wasn't ice cream as we know it today. It was a kind of frozen food exported into ancient Rome. In the 13th century, a recipe for making milk sherbet circulated around Europe, allegedly brought back from China by Marco Polo. In the 16th century, the Italians created what they called "water ice." Later, this somehow evolved into ice cream and spread to France, Britain, and America.

Originally, ice cream was mainly a dessert for the rich and royal of Europe. Even in democratic America, it didn't become available to the general public until 1832, when the first ice cream shop opened in Philadelphia. As for the popular ice cream cone, no one knows for certain when this came into being. Paper and metal cones were used to serve ice cream in France and Britain in the late 18th century. Some food historians say the first edible cone was cooked up in England in the 1850s. American food historians claim it made its first appearance in 1904, at the St. Louis World's Fair.

As Americans are fond of saying, I scream, you scream, we all scream for ice cream. Today, there are literally thousands of different ice cream flavors to satisfy every individual and cultural taste. On a hot summer's day, what flavor do you scream for?

No.1 Who does tradition say invented ice cream?
No.2 When was a recipe for milk sherbet introduced into Europe?
No.3 When did the first ice cream shop open in America?
No.4 Where were paper and metal cones used to serve ice cream?
No.5 Who claims ice cream cone first appeared at the St. Luis World's Fair?

Chapter 9-1
接続詞（1）

1. 等位接続詞（1）
1) Jack **and** Jill went to the movies yesterday.
2) He is old, **but** he is still strong.
3) It is late, **so** you had better go home soon.
4) Get up at once, **and** you will catch the bus.
5) Study harder, **or** you will not succeed.
6) It may rain soon, **for** it is getting cloudy.

2. 「時」、「条件」を表す従属接続詞（1）
7) **When** he arrived home, it began to rain.
8) I usually jog a few miles **before** I have breakfast.
9) **As soon as** he came home, his mother went out.
10) Please wait **till** she **comes** back.
11) **If** it **rains** tomorrow, I won't go out.
　　※ 時、条件を表す副詞節では、未来のことでも現在形で表す。

3. 「譲歩」、「原因・理由」などを表す従属接続詞（1）
12) **Though** she is very tired, she has something to do tonight.
13) Why did you scold him? — **Because** he told a lie.
14) **Since** I didn't know the answer, I kept silent.
15) I'm glad **that** he won first prize at the exhibition.

4. 名詞節を導く従属接続詞（1）
16) I think **that** this is our teacher's house.
17) He said **that** his room was too small.
18) The fact is **that** I don't like vegetables.
19) I'm sure **that** you will get well soon.

5. その他の従属接続詞（1）
20) He is so tall **that** he can touch the ceiling.
21) Get up **as** early **as you can**.
22) Do **as** you like.
23) I am taller **than** Alice is.

Exercises

A. （　）内に入る適語を下の語群から選び、書き入れなさい。
1. She was poor, (　　) she was happy.
2. Let's go home (　　) it gets dark.
3. "(　　) is he crying?" "(　　) he lost his pet dog."
4. I am sorry (　　) I cannot help you.
　　　[but, though, before, because, that, why]

B. 次の各組の文が同じ意味になるように（　）内に適語を入れなさい。
1. ｛ He is very old, but he works hard.
　　(　　) he is very old, he works hard.
2. ｛ Run, and you'll catch the bus.
　　(　　) you run, you'll catch the bus.
3. ｛ She was so busy that she couldn't attend the meeting.
　　She was (　　) busy (　　) attend the meeting.

C. 次の日本文を英文に直しなさい。
1. 私は鍵をなくしたので、この自転車を使うことはできません。

2. できるだけ早くここへ来てください。

3. 彼が来るまでここで待っていてください。

4. 彼は病気ではないかと心配です。

Exercises

D. 次の英文を読み、それに続く質問に英語で答えなさい。

Vending Machines

Japan is well known for its vending machines. In fact, it could be called the vending machine capital of the world. No matter where you are in Japan, you're only a step or two away from a vending machine. Streets and buildings are overflowing with them. Thirsty? Oh, there's a hot and cold drinks machine right there. This is definitely not the case in most other countries, though. You seldom see a vending machine in public places. Japanese, when they travel abroad, often find this lack of vending machines very inconvenient.

Why have vending machines become so popular in Japan? Limited space, the dense population, and low crime rate have all been pointed out as reasons.

Behind the convenience of Japan's vending machines lie some serious problems. Some sell cigarettes and beer, so even teenagers can readily buy them. Vending machines also raise concerns about the environment. Critics say they consume too much energy and waste resources. And, if you ask me, they're ugly, too.

No.1 Why could Japan be called the vending machine capital of the world?

No.2 When Japanese travel abroad what do they find inconvenient?

No.3 Why are some vending machines bad for teenagers?

No.4 How do vending machines affect the environment, according to some critics?

Chapter 9-2

接続詞（2）

1. 等位接続詞（2）

1) **Both** his father **and** mother are dead.
2) **Either** you **or** he must go there.
3) **Not only** he **but also** I am interested in the book.
4) That old man can **neither** read **nor** write.

2. 名詞節を導く従属接続詞（2）

5) Please advise me **whether** I should accept the offer.
6) Is **it** true **that** he has gone to Britain?
7) He asked me **if** I liked coffee.
8) We cannot deny the fact **that** smoking leads to cancer.

3. 「時」、「条件」を表す従属接続詞（2）

9) Strike **while** the iron is hot.
10) **The moment** she went out, he opened the letter.
11) They have been happy **since** they got married.
12) You mustn't enter the room **unless** I give you permission.
13) **In case** it rains, you should take an umbrella with you.
14) **Once** he decides, he won't change his mind.

4. 「譲歩」、「原因・理由」を表す従属接続詞（2）

15) **Even if** she comes, I won't see her.
16) **Whether** you walk or drive, you have only to arrive there in time.
17) Child **as** she was, she was brave.
18) You must **not** despise a man just **because** he is poor.
19) **Now that** you are well, we can eat out tonight.

5. その他の従属接続詞（2）

20) Study harder **so that** you **can** pass the examination.
21) He worked hard **in order that** he might support his large family.
22) Walk quietly **lest** you **should** wake up the baby.
23) He must be mad **that** he should say such a thing.
24) She talks **as if** she knew everything.
25) **As far as** I know, he has never studied abroad.

Exercises

A. （　）内に入る適語を下の語群から選び、書き入れなさい。
1. I didn't go to school, (　) I had a headache.
2. She called on me (　) I was out.
3. The rumor (　) she ran into trouble seems to be true.
4. (　) she grew older, she became more beautiful.
5. He treats me as (　) I were a little boy.

　　　[and, if, as, because, that, while]

B. 次の各組の文が同じ意味になるように（　）内に適語を入れなさい。
1. ⎰ She is not only beautiful but also clever.
   ⎱ She is clever as (　) as beautiful.
2. ⎰ I am sure that he will come soon.
   ⎱ I am sure (　) his coming soon.
3. ⎰ As soon as he left home, it began to rain.
   ⎱ No (　) had he left home than it began to rain.
4. ⎰ Whenever I called on him, I found him at work.
   ⎱ I never called on him (　) finding him at work.
5. ⎰ Though it was raining, we decided to go out.
   ⎱ In (　) of the rain, we decided to go out.

C. 次の各文を（　）内の指示に従って書き換えなさい。
1. She was taken ill. She has been weak from that time.（接続詞を用いて一文に）
2. She walked as quietly as possible so that he might not wake up.（lestを用いて）
3. The woman wept at the sight of her long-lost son.（接続詞を用いて）
4. He ran away so as not to be seen.（for that～を用いて）

D. 次の日本文を英文に直しなさい。
1. トムは子供の頃、日本に住んでいました。
2. 彼は、家族を養うために一生懸命働いています。
3. 君は頭がよいからといって勉強を怠ってはいけません。
4. 彼はどんなに忙しかろうと週に一度は家に手紙を書きます。
5. やっと一年経つか経たないうちにまた戦争が起こりました。（hardlyを用いて）

Exercises

E. 次の英文を読み、それに続く質問に英語で答えなさい。

Energetic Efforts for Energy

Not too long ago, a new type of gasoline went on sale at some gas stations in metropolitan areas in Japan. This new product, called biogasoline, is a mixture of gasoline and bioethanol. Bioethanol is made from plants, particularly corn and sugar cane. Brazil is one of the most advanced countries in the use of this new fuel. While Japanese biogasoline contains only 3% bioethanol, its Brazilian counterpart contains more than 20% bioethanol. Some gas stations in Brazil even offer 100% bioethanol.

The reason the use of biogasoline is spreading around the world is that it is expected to help protect the environment by decreasing CO_2 emissions. While very promising, this new fuel carries some problems. For example, some people doubt whether it really is effective in cutting carbon dioxide emissions. Others are concerned that increased biogasoline production could give rise to food shortages and higher food prices. In Mexico, corn flour, a staple of the diet, has already jumped in price.

Every coin has two sides. What is beneficial in one way may be harmful in another. What helps one person may hurt another. But we should not give up our energetic efforts to find steady, cheap, clean-burning sources of energy. As former U.S. Vice-president Al Gore says: "Our will to take action is itself a renewable resource."

No.1 What is bioethanol produced from?

No.2 What percentage of bioethanol does Japanese biogasoline have?

No.3 What is the purpose behind using biogasoline?

No.4 What has happened in Mexico?

No.5 What do we need to find?

Chapter 10-1
前置詞（1）

1. at（1）
 1) We have breakfast **at** seven.（時の一点）
 2) She saw him **at** the station.（場所の一点）

2. by（1）
 3) You must come home **by** nine o'clock.（期限）
 4) I go to school **by** train.（交通手段）

3. for（1）
 5) He wants to work **for** world peace.（目的・追求）
 6) It has been raining **for** more than five hours.（期間）

4. from（1）
 7) How far is it **from** here to your school?（起点）
 8) Where do you come **from**?（出身）

5. in（1）
 9) Tom lives **in** Kyoto.（場所・位置）
 10) I will be back **in** an hour.（経過時間）

6. of（1）
 11) I am a member **of** the tennis club.（所属）
 12) This desk is made **of** wood.（材料）

7. on（1）
 13) There is a world map **on** the wall.（接触）
 14) My father is at home **on** Sundays.（曜日・日付）

8. to（1）
 15) She went **to** France last year.（到達点）
 16) We should be kind **to** old people.（関係）

9. with（1）
 17) I usually go to school **with** Akio.（同伴）
 18) I eat **with** chopsticks.（道具）

10. その他の前置詞（1）
 19) They went **out of** the room.（外向運動）
 20) She ran **into** the classroom.（内向運動）
 21) I waited for her **till** seven o'clock.（継続）
 22) There are five bridges **over** the river.（真上）
 23) The cat **under** the tree is Lucy's.（真下）
 24) I will go to the United States **during** the summer vacation.（特定の期間中）

Exercises

A. 次の英文の（　）内から適語を選びなさい。
1. You must write (at, in, with) black ink.
2. There is a fly (on, above, under) the ceiling.
3. Wait here (by, for, till) five o'clock.
4. Father will come back (at, in, by) an hour.
5. There is a bridge (on, over, from) the river.

B. 次の英文の（　）内に適当な前置詞を入れなさい。
1. This building is made (　) brick.
2. Taro was born (　) the morning of January 1.
3. He was staying (　) a hotel (　) Chicago.
4. Who are you waiting (　)?
5. She bought a doll (　) twenty dollars.

C. 次の英文を日本文に直しなさい。
1. The sun has just risen above the horizon.
2. Some people die from some unknown causes.
3. Her mother looks very young for her age.
4. He is very familiar with Japanese history.
5. At this time of the year it is coldest here.

D. 次の日本文を英文に直しなさい。
1. 学校は４月に始まります。
2. 明日までにはこの仕事を仕上げます。
3. 彼女は飛行機で世界中を旅行しました。(travelを用いて)
4. 彼は一言も言わずに部屋を出て行きました。
5. あなたの出身地はどこですか。

Exercises

E. 次の英文を読み、それに続く質問に英語で答えなさい。No.1,2は適語を選びなさい。

For students enrolled in my Introduction to Economics class

The deadline for turning (1) your term papers for this class is Friday, November 20, at 5 p.m. So you have exactly two weeks left to wrap things up. You can either hand in a hard copy of your paper to my secretary, or, better yet, you can send me an e-mail with your paper attached. If you still have questions about your paper and would like to discuss it with me, come and see me in my office during my office hours on the third floor of the John Maynard Keynes Building. However, I must inform you that I will be absent Monday (2) Wednesday of next week because of research activities. I will be available for consultation on Thursday and Friday, and most of the following week, though I hope by then you will no longer need me!

Dr. Fritz Burns
Friday, November 6

Note: wrap up：まとめ上げる、書き上げる

No.1 Choose the best word for the blank (1).
　　(a) for　　(b) to　　(c) in

No.2 Choose the best word for the blank (2).
　　(a) at　　(b) for　　(c) through

No.3 How would the teacher prefer students to submit their papers?

No.4 Why will the professor be absent?

Chapter 10-2
前置詞（2）

1. いろいろな前置詞（2）

1) Ben threw a stone **at** the dog.（目標）
2) We are still hard **at** work.（従事）
3) Alex is older than Dave **by** three years.（差異の程度）
4) They flew to the UK **by** Copenhagen.（経路 = by way of）
5) Are you **for** or against the proposal?（賛成）
6) New York is famous **for** its skyscrapers.（理由）
7) **From** the look on her face, we could tell that she was lying.（判断の根拠）
8) Most of the students were tired **from** the hike.（原因）
9) We sat singing **in** a circle on the floor.（形状）
10) All the boys were **in** uniform.（着用）
11) Our town is about 30 miles to the south **of** Kyoto.（位置の分離）
12) Do you believe in the existence **of** ghosts?（主格関係）
13) The workers in the factory are **on** strike.（状態）
14) This novel is based **on** facts.（根拠）
15) They were dancing **to** soft music.（適合・一致）
16) **To** my surprise, I found the house empty.（結果）
17) The weather had something to do **with** that accident.（関係・関連）
18) How far can you walk **with** your eyes closed?（付帯状況）

2. 前置詞の後置

19) **What** are you blaming me **for**?
20) I want **something** to write **with**.
21) This building has no **room** for me to study **in**.

3. 群前置詞

22) **According to** the newspaper, there was an earthquake in Hokkaido.
23) **As for** the trip, we'll discuss it at the next meeting.
24) I didn't go out **because of** the typhoon.
25) This car runs **by means of** electricity.
26) Her success was **due to** diligence.
27) She went to Paris **for the purpose of** studying art.
28) We enjoyed our holidays **in spite of** the bad weather.

4. 二重前置詞

29) Our cat came **from behind** the curtain.
30) We went on talking **until after** midnight.

Exercises

A. 次の英文の（　）内に適当な前置詞を入れなさい。
1. I felt in my pocket (　　) the key.
2. He failed in his enterprise because (　　) lack of courage.
3. They lifted the stone (　　) means of a lever.
4. She went to London (　　) the purpose of studying.

B. 文末の日本語を参考にして（　）内に適語を入れなさい。
1. She had to take (　　)(　　) her parents.（面倒を見る）
2. You must not speak (　　)(　　) others behind their backs.（悪口をいう）
3. They have been looking (　　)(　　) the summer holidays.（期待する）
4. You must not find (　　)(　　) others.（あら捜しをする）

C. 下線部に入る適当な語句を下から選びなさい。
1. ＿＿＿＿＿ me, I like summer best of all the seasons.
2. I stayed at home ＿＿＿＿＿ the heavy rain.
3. They succeeded ＿＿＿＿＿ all difficulties.
4. We have a lot of news ＿＿＿＿＿ the sea.
   〔a) in spite of　b) on account of　c) from over　d) as for〕

D. 次の英文を日本文に直しなさい。
1. He has been living there since before the war.
2. His eldest brother was given up for lost.
3. The doctor was mistaken for an assistant.
4. I can't write anything with you standing there.

E. 次の日本文を英文に直しなさい。
1. 彼は米原経由で金沢に行きました。

2. 彼は通りの向こうから私を呼びました。

3. 学校は駅から約2マイル離れたところにあります。

4. 両手をポケットに入れたまま話をしてはいけません。

Exercises

F. 次の英文を読み、それに続く質問に英語で答えなさい。

A Moral Problem

Public littering has become a major problem in our country. Everywhere we go we can see household trash and food scraps, plastic bottles and metal cans, electrical appliances, bicycles, and even large pieces of machinery scattered and dumped in plain sight. This waste smells bad, pollutes our waterways, blocks our roads, and ruins the landscape. It also poses a serious threat to our security and health.

Of course, there are strict laws and rules against such illegal dumping, and there are local and national government systems and facilities for handling waste matter of all kinds. But some people ignore the laws and rules. They refuse to go along with the system and to use the designated waste treatment facilities. In other words, they lack the sense of public morality and responsibility that every good citizen should have.

Why would people do such a thing? There are several explanations. Dumping garbage illegally is easier, less time consuming, and less expensive than taking care of it properly. Moreover, some people actually make money out of illegal waste handling. Whatever the reason, such people either do not realize or do not care that they are causing great damage to society and nature. And to make matters worse, they are seldom caught and punished for their actions. Naturally, the police, government and other law enforcement agencies have the right and duty to control the situation. But we, as individual citizens, must also obey the rules and do our part to protect our daily living environment.

No.1 What has become a major problem in our country?
No.2 What does waste pose?
No.3 What do some people who ignore the laws and rules lack?
No.4 Why do some people dump garbage illegally?
No.5 What must we do to protect our living environment?

Chapter 11-1

形容詞・副詞 (1)

1. 形容詞の用法 (1)

1) 限定用法

Alice is a **diligent** girl.

I want something **hot** to drink.

2) 叙述用法

My uncle looks **young** for his age.

This apartment is **comfortable** to live in.

2. 形容詞の語順

| 冠詞類 | → | 序数 | → | 数量 | → | 性状 | → | 大小・形状 | → | 色・新旧 | → | 材料・所属 | | 名 詞 |

3) Look at **that pretty young French** girl.

4) Would you try **these first ripe big** apples?

5) Roy bought **a new gray steel** desk.

3. 数量形容詞 (1)

6) **Many** old people were at the meeting.

7) How **much** snow do you have here in winter?

8) I have **a few** pen pals in the United Kingdom.

9) There is **little** hope of her recovery.

4. 副詞の用法 (1)

10) Ben studies English very **hard**. (動詞を修飾)

11) She was **very** late for school yesterday. (形容詞を修飾)

12) He drives **too** carefully. (他の副詞を修飾)

5. 副詞の位置

13) 形容詞・副詞を修飾する場合：ふつう被修飾語の前

You're **quite** right.

She plays the harp **very** well.

14) 動詞を修飾する場合

① 頻度・否定を表す副詞の場合

She **sometimes** comes to see us. (一般動詞の場合はその前)

He is **usually** free on Saturdays. (be動詞・助動詞の場合はその後)

② 様態を表す副詞の場合

Jill lived **happily** with Jack. (自動詞の場合はその後)

She will answer the questions **easily**. (他動詞の場合はふつう目的語の後)

③ 時と場所を表す副詞がある場合：ふつう場所の副詞が先

There was a traffic accident **here yesterday**.

Exercises

A. 次の英文の（　）内から適当な語句を選びなさい。
1. In Japan we have (many, much) rain in June.
2. His wife cooks very (good, well).
3. It is raining very (hardly, hard).
4. He doesn't have (some, any) money with him.
5. There is (a few, a little) milk in the bottle.

B. 次の英文を例にならって書き換えなさい。
　［例］She plays the piano very well. ⇔ She is a very good pianist.
1. Henry speaks very carefully.

2. Betty is a very hard worker.

3. She can speak English very well.

C. （　）内の語を正しく並べかえなさい。
1. (must, clean, you, your, keep, room).

2. (Bill, for, late, sometimes, is, school).

3. (kind, was, the, very, girl, us, to).

4. (an, told, story, interesting, he, us).

D. 次の日本文を英文に直しなさい。
1. 彼女は彼よりも金持ちです。

2. あなたは古い切手を持っていますか。

3. 私は日曜日はいつも家にいます。

4. 鳥たちが楽しそうに歌っていました。

Exercises

E. 次の英文を読み、それに続く質問では、それぞれの書き出しに続けるのに最も適切なものを選びなさい。

A New Bride

My uncle had been married to his first wife for nearly twenty years and was still deeply in love with her when she died of cancer in 2000. So why did he choose to get married again? The answer is simple: his new bride is a pretty amazing person.

She had a very rough childhood and left home when she was barely in her teens. By the time she was fourteen, she was already living on her own. For a time, you could even say she was homeless! But she was also quite beautiful and very ambitious. She entered a modeling contest, and won it hands down. Before long she began working as a professional model and soon started her own agency. It was at a fashion event that she happened to meet my uncle. They were charmed by each other and decided to "tie the knot."

Note: win hands down：楽勝する

No.1 The writer's uncle was married to his previous wife
- (a) for over twenty years.
- (b) for under twenty years.
- (c) for just twenty years.

No.2 The writer's uncle decided to get married again because his new wife
- (a) resembles his former wife.
- (b) has lots of money.
- (c) is a wonderful person.

No.3 When the new bride was a teenager, she
- (a) earned her own living.
- (b) had a rough childhood.
- (c) worked with homeless people.

No.4 When the writer's uncle first met his new bride,
- (a) she was in a beauty contest.
- (b) she was running a modeling agency.
- (c) she was homeless.

Chapter 11-2
形容詞・副詞（2）

1. 形容詞の用法（2）
  1) 限定用法のみ：**only**, **elder**, **entire**, **mere**, **main**, **total**, etc.
     This boy is her **only** child.
     What are the **main** points of your speech?
  2) 叙述用法のみ：**afraid**, **alike**, **alive**, **alone**, **asleep**, **awake**, **aware**, **subject**, **well**, etc.
     I was happy to hear that the old man was still **alive**.
     He is **subject** to stomachaches.
  3) 用法により意味が異なるもの：**certain**, **due**, **late**, **present**, etc.
     He meets her at a **certain** place in Osaka once a month.「ある（決まった）」
     She is **certain** of his success.「確信して」
     They are not satisfied with the **present** cabinet.「現在の」
     Was Mr. Sakai **present** at the party?「出席して」

2. 形容詞＋前置詞
  4) I am **familiar with** this part of Fukuoka.
  5) He is **anxious for** fame and fortune.
  6) She is **keen on** collecting stamps.

3. 形容詞＋to-不定詞
  7) It's **likely to** be cold here in winter.
  8) They are **eager to** climb Mt. Fuji.
  9) Matthew is **liable to** lose his temper.

4. 形容詞＋that-節/wh-節
  10) She was **aware that** Ben was taking advantage of her.
  11) I'm not **sure where** he has gone.
  12) We are **positive that** things will come out right.

5. 数量形容詞（2）
  13) **Not a few** people believe in astrology.
  14) Teachers should spend **quite a little** time in preparing their lessons.
  15) There are **a large number of** colleges and universities in this area.

6. 副詞の用法（2）
  16) I was **quite** at a loss for words when he asked me to marry him.（句を修飾）
  17) We are happy **only** when we are healthy.（節を修飾）
  18) **Clearly** he came back here. = It was clear that he came back here.（文全体を修飾）
  19) I'm **quite** a stranger here.（名詞を修飾）
  20) **Only** you can help her.（代名詞を修飾）

Exercises

A. 次の各文の適当な位置に（　）内の語を入れなさい。

1. Tom can swim faster than John.（much）
2. I could believe my eyes at the sight.（hardly）
3. I am aware of the danger.（well）
4. A child can answer such an easy question.（even）
5. What did you do this morning?（else）

B. （　）内の語を正しく並べかえなさい。

1. This (to, of, me, is, book, no use).

2. The (school, hurry, girl, a, in, left).

3. He (every, our, day, comes, to, other, house).

4. I (off, airport, to, to, him, went, see, the).

5. His (largely, due, is, good, to, success, luck).

C. 次の各文の（　）内に適語を入れなさい。［5.の（　）内は同一語］

1. He solved the problem (　) ease.
2. She is old (　) to know how to behave.
3. "(　) did you come here?" "I came here by car."
4. "How (　) did you see him?" "I saw him twice a week."
5. Whatever is (　) doing at all is (　) doing well.

D. 次の日本文を英文に直しなさい。

1. 彼女は月に一度両親に手紙を書きます。

2. その学生は車を買えるほどのお金を稼ぎました。

3. 君はいつどこで鈴木先生に会ったのですか。

4. 幸運にも彼は死にませんでした。

5. 今日の新聞に何かおもしろいことが載っていますか。

Exercises

E. 次の英文を読み、それに続く質問に英語で答えなさい。

Global Warming

Every year, the earth is getting warmer and warmer. As the temperature rises, many unusual phenomena are appearing. Worldwide climates are changing. In some places there is too much rain, in others too little. Summers everywhere are getting hotter. This is causing the polar ice caps to melt, which, in turn, will lead to rising sea levels and flooding. If this trend continues, scientists say, our living environment could be destroyed by the end of the 21st century. Some low-lying islands and coastal areas could sink. Water wells could dry up. Deserts could expand, destroying land for raising food crops. Many animal and plant species could die out. Unless we take action immediately, these and many other dreadful consequences await us in the not too distant future.

Most experts agree that carbon dioxide emissions from fossil fuel-burning automobiles and factories are the primary factor behind this global warming. Although the Kyoto Protocol was put into effect to limit carbon dioxide emissions worldwide, it is not yet functioning sufficiently to achieve its original purpose and goal. This is mainly because the United States, a major emitter of carbon dioxide, has not ratified the Protocol. Meanwhile, more and more developing countries are progressing economically and are demanding the right to use automobiles for their transportation needs.

But we shouldn't let these anti-Kyoto Protocol trends blind us to what we need to see: that reducing carbon dioxide emissions and halting global warming are of life-and-death importance to us. International cooperation and the development of new energy sources that will free us from our dependence on fossil fuels are vital to stop global warming.

Note: the Kyoto Protocol：二酸化炭素の排出規制策を打ち出した「京都議定書」

No.1 What is happening to the earth every year?

No.2 What do scientists say about our living environment?

No.3 What is the primary factor behind global warming?

No.4 Why isn't the Kyoto Protocol functioning sufficiently?

No.5 What do we need to free us from our dependence on fossil fuels?

Chapter 12-1
比較（1）

1. 原級を用いた比較表現（1）: as ～ as... 「…と同じくらい～」

1) Fred is **as** old **as** Harry.
2) She is **not as** tall **as** her sister. 「…ほど～ない」
3) This boat is **three times as** big **as** that one. 「…の３倍～」
    = This boat is **three times the** size **of** that one.
4) Tom works **as** hard **as** he **can**. 「できるだけ～」
    = Tom works **as** hard **as possible**.
5) Our town has **as many** people **as** yours.
6) I spent **as much** money **as** he in the amusement park yesterday.
7) Ned read **twice as many** books **as** I last month.

2. 比較級を用いた比較表現（1）: ～er（more～）than ... 「…より～」

8) Davis is **taller than** his brother.
9) Dogs are **more useful than** cats.
10) Alice can play tennis **much better than** I. 「…よりずっと上手に～」
    ※ 他に比較級を強める語句には **far, a lot, even** などがある。
11) There are **many more** pigs **than** people there.（複数形の名詞を伴って）「…よりずっと多い～」
12) Tokyo is **larger than any other** city in Japan.
    = Tokyo is the largest of all the cities in Japan.
13) Her car is **less** expensive **than** mine. 「…ほど～ない」
    = Her car is not as expensive as mine.
14) It is getting **colder and colder**. 「だんだん～」

3. 最上級を用いた比較表現（1）: the ～est（the most ～）「いちばん～」

15) This is **the oldest** building in our town.
16) Lucy is **the most beautiful** of the five women.
17) She is **happiest** when she has a date with Tom.
    ※ 同一人（物）に関する比較のときはtheをつけない。
18) Bill is **by far the best** student in his class.
    ※ 他に最上級を強める語句には、**much**（much the best）, **very**（the very best）などがある。
19) That is **the second tallest** building in the city.
20) Soccer is **one of the most popular** sports here.

Exercises

A. 次の英文の（　）内から適当な語句を選びなさい。
1. Taro looks (young, younger, the youngest) than Bill.
2. Which do you like (much, well, better), tea or coffee?
3. I can't speak French as (well, better, best) as Dick.
4. He studies (hard, harder, hardest) of the five.

B. （　）内の語を正しく並べかえなさい。
1. Light travels (than, much, faster) sound.
2. Mt. Fuji is (other, higher, any, than) mountain in Japan.
3. This is (terrible, far, the, by, most) experience I have ever had.
4. I want to read (many, as, as, books) I can.

C. 次の英文を日本文に直しなさい。
1. This box is five times as heavy as that one.

2. I ran as fast as possible.

3. He speaks English more fluently than she.

4. The story became more and more interesting.

5. This is one of the tallest buildings in the city.

D. 次の日本文を英文に直しなさい。
1. 私は彼の2倍の切手をもっています。

2. 彼は彼女より五つ年上です。

3. この湖はここが一番深いです。

4. 銀は金ほど重くありません。(lessを用いて)

5. ケイト (Kate) はクラスの他のどの生徒よりも早く学校にやって来ます。

Exercises

E. 次の英文を読み、No.1, 2, 4は質問に対する最も適切な答を、No.3は書き出しに続けるのに最も適切なものを選びなさい。

How Many Books Do You Have?

There is a very comfortable study in our house. It is my favorite room, a place where I can escape to and read and study in peace and quiet. Or go to just to think and relax. The room is full of books. My grandfather, who died last month at the age of 80, was a real book lover. He collected books all his life. My father loves books, too. He has as many books as my grandfather. As for me, well, I'm still young, so I don't have all that many books yet. My father is proud of the fact that he has three times as many books as I have. But now I'm going to inherit all my grandfather's books. Then I will have more books than my father.

No.1 What is the study?
  (a) It's a room for entertainment.
  (b) It's a room with lots of books.
  (c) It's a person who studies.

No.2 How many studies are there in the writer's house?
  (a) One.
  (b) Two.
  (c) Three.

No.3 Before the writer's grandfather died, the writer had
  (a) as many books as his father.
  (b) half as many books as his father.
  (c) one third as many books as his father.

No.4 Now who is going to have the most books?
  (a) The writer.
  (b) The writer's father.
  (c) The writer's grandfather.

Chapter 12-2
比較（2）

1. 原級を用いた比較表現（2）：as～as ...「…と同じくらい～」

1) **No other** boy in this class is **as** tall **as** Tom.「他のどんな―も…ほど～ない」
2) Ben studies **as** hard **as any** student in this school.「どんな…にも劣らず～」
3) Joanne is **as** kind **as** she is wise.「…でもあり～でもある」
    Cf. She is **as** happy **as**（happy）**can be**.
4) Mr. Yoshida is **not so much** a teacher **as** a scholar.「～というよりむしろ…」
    = Mr. Yoshida is a scholar **rather than** a teacher.
    Cf. He **cannot so much as** write his own name.「～さえできない」
5) He works **as** hard **as ever**.「相変わらず～」
    Cf. He is **as** great a chef **as ever lived**.「古今を通じて最も～」
6) Any book will do **as long as** it is interesting.「…する限り」
7) He is **as good as** dead.「…（した）も同然」
8) He made five mistakes in **as many** lines.「同数の～（つまりこの場合はfive）」
9) You **might as well** die **as** go there.「…するくらいなら～する方がましだ」
    Cf. You **might as well** stay in bed.「～する方がよいだろう」

2. 比較級を用いた比較表現（2）：～er（more～）than...「…より～」

10) He is **the taller of the two**.「二者のうちで～な方」
11) **The higher** we go, **the colder** it becomes.「～すればするほど、ますます…」
12) A whale is **no more** a fish **than** a horse is.「―は…と同様に～ではない」
13) She is three years **senior**［**junior**］**to** me.「…より年上［年下］」
14) She is **more** cute **than** beautiful.「…というよりはむしろ～」
15) She has **no less than**［**no more than, not less than, not more than**］100 dollars with her.「～も［たった～、少なくとも～、せいぜい～］」
16) He can speak French, **much more** English.「まして～はなおさらだ」
17) He **knows better than to** fight against such a rascal.「～するほど愚かではない」
18) I had **no sooner** closed my eyes **than** the telephone rang.「～するやいなや…」

3. 最上級を用いた比較表現（2）：the～est（the most～）「いちばん～」

19) **The wisest** man sometimes nods.「最も…な～でさえ（= Even the …est～）」
20) She is **a most** kind woman.「非常に～」Cf. most houses「たいていの～」
21) You should **make the most of** your opportunities.「～を最大限に利用する」
22) The cherry blossoms are **at their best** now.「見ごろで」
23) It does **not** matter **in the least**.「ちっとも～ない」
24) She is **the last** person I want to see.「最も…しそうにない～」
25) **To the best of** my knowledge, he is reliable.「～の限りでは」

Exercises

A. 次の各組の文が同じ意味になるように（　）内に適語を入れなさい。

1. { He is the (　　) speaker of English in our class.
   { (　　)(　　) student in our class speaks English better than he does.

2. { She can play the piano better than you.
   { She is (　　)(　　) you in playing the piano.

3. { She is not so much a scholar as a writer.
   { She is a writer (　　)(　　) a scholar.

4. { It was quite a surprise to see him there.
   { He was the (　　) man I expected to see there.

B 次の各文を（　）内の指示に従って書き換えなさい。

1. He is the most eloquent speaker of all.（Nobodyで始めて原級で）
2. He is less strong than any other boy.（最上級で）
3. I have never climbed a higher mountain than this.（最上級で）
4. I am your senior by three years.（thanを用いて）
5. Happiness is in contentment rather than in riches.（asを用いて）
6. As far as I know, he has never been there.（knowledgeを用いて）
7. Tom is inferior to Jim in speaking German.（speak, lessを用いて）
8. This city is half as populous as that one.（that cityを主語にし、largeを用いて）

C. 次の英文を日本文に直しなさい。

1. This pencil is the shorter of the two.
2. The more he talked, the less I understood.
3. No fewer than 100 houses were burnt down in the recent fire.
4. She spends money as freely as if she were a billionaire.
5. I have never seen him, much less talked with him.

D. 次の日本文を英文に直しなさい。

1. 彼より正直な人はいません。（比較級を用いて）

2. 平和ほど望ましいものはありません。（原級を用いて）

3. 彼女は使えないほどのお金を持っています。

Exercises

E. 次の英文を読み、それに続く質問に英語で答えなさい。

True Democracy

Japan is said to be a democratic country. Is this because our constitution guarantees every adult citizen the right to vote and to participate in the election of our representatives? Or is it because the constitution includes the concept of the balance of powers? Both may be true, and there may be lots of other factors as well. But we must remember that the most important thing in any democracy is how well the issues of the day are discussed and debated among the citizens. Of equal importance is how accurately the citizens' needs and opinions are reflected in the actions of representatives in local and national legislatures. This kind of political system is far better than those that do not allow their citizens free and open discussion.

All too often a democracy becomes the equivalent of majority rule. A political party that controls more than half the seats of a legislature possesses superior power and passes laws that it thinks best. This system has a serious defect, however. It tends to ignore minority voices. Minorities usually have valuable insights that the majority cannot or refuses to see. True democracy requires us to see the essence of any issue from various angles. True democracy takes the time to examine the issues thoroughly and conscientiously. True democracy calls for a balanced decision-making process in which everyone's voice is heard, respected, and reflected in local and national laws.

No.1 What does our constitution guarantee every adult citizen?
No.2 What is the most important thing in any democracy?
No.3 What is a serious defect of majority rule?
No.4 What does true democracy require us to do?
No.5 Why does true democracy call for a balanced decision-making process?

Chapter 13-1
不定詞（1）

1. 不定詞の基本的用法
1) 名詞的用法
To play here is dangerous.（主語として）
I want **to travel** abroad.（目的語として）
My dream is **to help** sick and poor people.（補語として）
2) 形容詞的用法
I have some friends **to support** me.
There is no one **to help** the greedy man in the world.
I want something **to drink**.
3) 副詞的用法
I got up early **to catch** the first train.（目的）
I am glad **to hear** the news.（原因・理由）
He awoke **to find** himself in a strange room.（結果）

2. 不定詞に関する基本事項および慣用表現
4) **It** is good for the health **to keep** early hours.（形式主語によって文尾に）
5) I found **it** difficult **to solve** the problem.（形式目的語によって文尾に）
6) Dave often **asks** me **to help** him with his homework.（目的語＋不定詞）
　＝ Dave often says to me, "Please help me with my homework."
7) Do you know **what to do** next?（疑問詞＋不定詞）
　＝ Do you know what you should do next?
8) She was **too tired to walk** any farther.
　＝ She was so tired that she couldn't walk any farther.
9) He is tall **enough to touch** the ceiling.
　＝ He is so tall that he can touch the ceiling.
10) He told me **not to open** the door.（不定詞の否定）
　＝ He said to me, "Don't open the door."
11) I never **heard** him **sing**.（知覚動詞の後の原形不定詞）
　→ He was never heard **to sing** by me.
12) They **made** me **work** all day long.（使役動詞の後の原形不定詞）
　→ I was made **to work** all day long.
13) You don't have to go there if you don't want **to**.（代不定詞）
　＝ You don't have to go there if you don't want **to go there**.
14) You **had better** start at once.「～するほうがいい」

Exercises

A. 次の英文を日本文に直しなさい。
1. There was no time to lose.
2. To get up early, you must go to bed early.
3. I found it difficult to do so.
4. Will you lend me something to write with?
5. He was very disappointed to hear the result.

B. 次の1.～3.の文中の不定詞と同じ用法のものを下から**2**つずつ選び、（　　）内にその記号を書きなさい。
1. His only fault is to talk too much. （　）（　）
2. Please give me something to drink. （　）（　）
3. I was surprised to hear the news of his death. （　）（　）

　　　a) Please come to see us next Sunday.
　　　b) He has no house to live in.
　　　c) Please teach me how to cook.
　　　d) It is my great pleasure to read books after supper.
　　　e) He grew up to be a great scientist.
　　　f) The best way to master English is practice.

C. 次の各組の文の意味が同じになるように（　　）内に適語を入れなさい。

1. { They saw her wash the dishes.
     She was （　　）（　　） wash the dishes.

2. { She said to her son, "Don't swim in the river."
     She told her son （　　）（　　） swim in the river.

3. { He is so rich that he can buy a yacht.
     He is rich （　　）（　　） buy a yacht.

4. { The dress is so expensive that she cannot buy it.
     The dress is （　　） expensive （　　） her （　　） buy.

D. 次の日本文を英文に直しなさい。
1. ここであなたにお会いしてたいへん嬉しいです。
2. 彼の仕事はバスを運転することです。
3. この部屋には座る椅子がありません。
4. この英語の辞書は使い易いです。
5. ピエロ（clown）は私たちを笑わせます。

Exercises

E. 次の英文を読み、それに続く質問にNo.1, 3は書き出しに続けるのに最も適切なものを、No.2は質問に対する最も適切な答を選び、No.4は英語で答えなさい。

Bold and Happy

One day a new girl walked into my English class in high school. Her name was Jane. As soon as I saw her, I wanted to ask her out. She was beautiful, kind, and funny. But in those days, I was the shy type. I wasn't socially skilled enough to go up to a girl and just start talking to her. So I kept putting off asking Jane for a date. I guess I was waiting for the perfect opportunity. But then I got tired of waiting.

One afternoon after school, I walked up to her, took a deep breath and dared to ask, "How about going to an amusement park with me on Saturday?" To my amazement, she said, "I'd love to." We went and had a very good time. After that we started "going steady." We often went to movies, concerts and dinner together. And, six years after that first date, Jane became my wife. Now we've been happily married going on ten years already. To be happy in life, it is sometimes necessary to be bold.

No.1 When the writer was a high school student, he could not openly talk with the girls
  (a) because he was so kind.
  (b) because he was so shy.
  (c) because he was so sophisticated.

No.2 Where did the writer go on his first date with Jane?
  (a) To an amusement park.
  (b) To a movie theater.
  (c) To a concert hall.

No.3 The writer's first date
  (a) was very successful.
  (b) ended in failure.
  (c) was canceled.

No.4 How long have the writer and Jane known each other?

Chapter 13-2 不定詞（2）

1. 不定詞の意味上の主語

1) **I** want **to do** it.
2) I want **you to do** it.
   Cf. **I** promise you **to come** back by ten o'clock.
3) It is impossible **for her to kill** even a worm.
   Cf. It is foolish **of her to say** such a thing.

2. 不定詞の表す時

4) She **seems to be** happy. = It **seems** that she **is** happy.
5) She **seemed to be** happy. = It **seemed** that she **was** happy.
6) He i**s said to have been** a doctor. = It **is said** that he **was** a doctor.
7) He **was said to have been** a doctor. = It **was said** that he **had been** a doctor.
8) 実現されなかった意図・期待
   He **wanted to have bought** it. = He **had wanted to buy** it.
   = He wanted to buy it, but he couldn't.

3. 独立不定詞

9) **To be frank with you**, I can't help you.
10) **To tell the truth**, she wrote the letter.
11) He is, **so to speak**, a walking dictionary.

4. Be to do

12) The ship **is to arrive** tomorrow.（予定）
13) No stars **were to be seen** last night.（可能）
14) You **are to report** to the police at once.（義務）
15) She **was never to see** her country again.（運命）
16) If you **are to succeed** in life, you must work hard.（意図）

5. 不定詞を含むその他の慣用表現等

17) I got up early **so as to** / **in order to** be in time for the first bus.（目的）
18) He is **so** rich **as to** buy anything he wants.（程度）
19) He tried it again, **only to fail**.（結果）
20) This river is dangerous **to swim** in.（限定）
21) I **happened to** sit next to Ms. Smith in the theater.「偶然〜した」
22) **Don't fail to** let me know when Sam comes.「必ず〜する」
23) He **came to** realize that she didn't love him.「〜するようになった」
24) It is time **to seriously consider** banning all smoking in public places.（分離不定詞）

Exercises

A. 次の英文を日本文に直しなさい。
1. He shed tears to see the sight.
2. I had him fix my broken cassette player.
3. The first thing for you to do is to gather the fallen leaves.
4. She was never to return to her own country.

B. 下線部に入る適当な語句を下から選びなさい。
1. ＿＿＿＿, I don't like to be with him.
2. He is, ＿＿＿＿, a self-made man.
3. ＿＿＿＿, he had the same dream twice last night.
4. ＿＿＿＿, his mother was taken ill.
5. He plays the piano, ＿＿＿＿ the guitar.

  a) so to speak   b) to say nothing of
  c) to be frank with you   d) to make matters worse
  e) strange to say

C. 次の各組の文が同じ意味になるように（ ）内に適語を入れなさい。

1. ⎰ He got a driver's license so that he might drive a car.
   ⎱ He got a driver's license (　　) (　　) (　　) drive a car.

2. ⎰ I think you are very strong and can lift this stone.
   ⎱ I think you are strong (　　) (　　) (　　) this stone.

3. ⎰ He intended to visit the museum, but he couldn't.
   ⎱ He intended (　　) (　　) (　　) the museum.

4. ⎰ She made me go on an errand.
   ⎱ I was (　　) (　　) (　　) on an errand by her.

5. ⎰ He seemed to have been idle when young.
   ⎱ It seemed that (　　) (　　) (　　) idle when young.

D. 次の日本文を英文に直しなさい。
1. そんなことを言うなんて、彼は気が狂っているに違いない。
2. まず第一に、私の少年時代のことをお話しましょう。
3. ご迷惑をおかけして申し訳ございません。
4. 家の鍵をなくすとは、君も迂闊でしたね。

Exercises

E. 次の英文を読み、それに続く質問に英語で答えなさい。

Reading and Traveling

How many people can you meet in one lifetime? How many experiences can you have? The answer to these questions varies from person to person. Generally speaking, though, most of us are destined to have far fewer encounters with people than we would like, and not nearly as many experiences. After all, life is short, and opportunities are limited. Yet one of the most important things in life is to meet as many new and fascinating people as we can, and to experience as many different things as possible. This helps us to gain a better understanding of human nature, gives us better insights into life, and allows us to evaluate things from various angles.

So how, despite limitations, can we meet new people and gain new experiences? One answer is to read as many books from various genres as possible, and to travel to as many different places as time and budget allow. Reading a good book is like getting to know a whole roomful of new people. A good book acquaints you with new and different ideas, introduces you to alternative opinions and ways of thinking, and expands your knowledge of the world. The same goes for travel. Travel opens you up to new cultures and ways of living, enabling you to broaden your perspectives on life and society. So whenever you can, pick up a good book, or book yourself a flight to somewhere exotic and exciting. You'll be a new person yourself.

No.1 Why can we meet only a limited number of people and experiences?
No.2 What is one of the most important things in life?
No.3 What is it like to read a good book?
No.4 What does travel do?
No.5 What will happen if you read a new book and travel to a new place?

Chapter 14-1
分詞（1）

A 分詞の限定用法

1. 現在分詞（前置）
1) Look at that **swimming** boy.
2) This **sleeping** boy is my brother.
3) A **drowning** man will catch at a straw.

2. 現在分詞（後置）
4) Do you know the man **sitting** on the bench?
5) The man **washing** a car is my father.
6) Who is the girl **standing** next to Della?

3. 過去分詞（前置）
7) Give me one of the **boiled** eggs.
8) The old building has many **broken** windows.
9) A **lost** chance will never come again.

4. 過去分詞（後置）
10) This is a story **written** by Soseki Natsume.
11) The dinner **cooked** by Father was very delicious.
12) She has a bag **made** in France.

B 分詞の叙述用法

5. 主格補語として
13) They came **running** into the classroom.
14) Dick stood **talking** with Beth in the train.
15) He looked **worried** about his health.
16) We got **interested** in flower arrangement.

6. 目的格補語（知覚動詞等＋目的語＋分詞）として（1）
17) I saw him **watering** the flowers.
18) I heard my name **called**.
19) He felt his heart **beating** wildly.
20) My brother found a poor dog **injured** in the woods.

Exercises

A. （　）内の語を正しい形に変え、下線部に書き入れなさい。
1. Who is that _____ boy?（cry）
2. There is a _____ watch on the desk.（break）
3. Look at the boy _____ in the river.（swim）
4. I have a car _____ in Germany.（make）
5. The dog came _____ across the street.（run）

B. （　）内の語を適当な形にしてア〜エのいずれかに入れなさい。
1. They（ア）stood（イ）for（ウ）the（エ）train.（wait）
2. The book（ア）by（イ）him（ウ）is（エ）very interesting.（write）
3. What are（ア）the（イ）languages（ウ）in（エ）Canada?（speak）
4. Who is（ア）the（イ）boy（ウ）with（エ）Alice?（talk）
5. I want（ア）to（イ）eat（ウ）some（エ）rice.（boil）

C. （　）内の語を正しく並べ替えなさい。
1. My (hear, surprised, news, father, the, looked, to).

2. The (aunt, chair, sitting, on, woman, is, my, the).

3. There (standing, the doorway, is, in, someone).

4. You (be, water, the, careful, boiling, must, with).

5. The (my father's, is, by, washed, car, Tom).

D. 次の英文を日本文に直しなさい。
1. They escaped from the burning house.

2. A rolling stone gathers no moss.

3. Canned food is very useful in case of emergency.

4. He showed me a letter written in French.

5. We remained looking at each other for a while.

Exercises

E. 次の英文を読み、それに続く質問に No.1, 3 は書き出しに続けるのに最も適切なものを、No.2, 4 は質問に対する最も適切な答を選びなさい。

Who Is J. K. Rowling?

I don't think there's anyone who hasn't heard of Harry Potter. The Harry Potter books are probably the most popular series of novels in history. They have been translated into dozens of different languages. It seems that everyone in the world over loves Harry Potter. I'm sure you've read at least some of the Harry Potter books, too.

But did you know that Harry's creator, J.K. Rowling, is as interesting a character as her young hero? Until the mid-1990s, no one had heard of J.K. Rowling. She was a recently divorced single mother trying to raise her infant daughter in Scotland on very little money. But she had a story in her head and a dream of writing it. She wrote her first book in a local café because it was more comfortable than her flat. She would order a cup of coffee and start writing away, with her daughter sleeping beside her.

Needless to say, J.K. Rowling's life has changed greatly thanks to Harry Potter. She is one of the world's richest women. In the summer of 2007 she completed the Harry Potter cycle, so I wonder what she will come up with next.

No.1 When she began to write the first Harry Potter book, Rowling lived in
(a) the United States.   (b) the U.K.   (c) London.

No.2 How many children did Rowling have at the time?
(a) One.   (b) Two.   (c) Three.

No.3 Rowling wrote her first book at a café
(a) because she wanted a cup of coffee.
(b) because she loved the atmosphere
(c) because she was more comfortable there than at home.

No.4 How many languages has the Harry Potter book been translated into?
(a) A few.   (b) More than ten.
(c) Hundreds.

Chapter 14-2 分詞 (2)

1. 目的格補語（使役動詞等＋目的語＋分詞）として (2)

1) Can you **make** yourself **understood** in English?
2) The comedian **had** them all **laughing**.
3) I would like to **have** / **get** my hair **cut**.
4) He **got** the engine **going**.
5) She **kept** me **waiting** long.

2. 注意すべき分詞

6) The game was **exciting**.
7) We were **excited** at the game.

3. 分詞構文

8) **Admitting** what you say, I still think that you are wrong.
　= Though I admit what you say, I still think that you are wrong.
9) **Not knowing** what to say, I kept silent.
　= Since I didn't know what to say, I kept silent.
10) **Having finished** her homework, she went to bed.
　= After she had finished her homework, she went to bed.

4. 受動態の分詞構文

11) **Left** alone, the little girl began to cry.
　= Because the little girl was left alone, she began to cry.
12) **Deceived** so often, she is on her guard.
　= As she has been deceived so often, she is on her guard.

5. 独立分詞構文 (1)

13) **The door closed**, they began to talk secretly.
　= When the door was closed, they began to talk secretly.
14) **All the money having been spent**, he went to work again.
　= As all the money had been spent, he went to work again.

6. 独立分詞構文 (2) … 慣用的に意味上の主語が省かれるもの

15) **Generally speaking**, the Japanese are an industrious people.
　= If we speak generally, the Japanese are an industrious people.
16) **Judging from** his clothes, he must be rich.
　= If we judge (him) from his clothes, he must be rich.

7. 付帯状況を表す

17) She was very happy, **surrounded** by many children.
18) He left the car, **with the engine running**.

Exercises

A. （ ）内の語を正しい形に変え、下線部に書き入れなさい。

1. She had her purse _____ in the _____ train. (steal, crowd)
2. I spent the morning _____ English. (study)
3. _____ from the plane, the mountain is very beautiful. (see)
4. Strictly _____ , this is different from that. (speak)

B. 次の各組の文が同じ意味になるように（　）内に適語を入れなさい。

1. {As it snowed last night, we warmed ourselves by a heater.
   Because (　) was (　) last night, we warmed ourselves by a heater.
2. {Because his arm was injured, he could not write.
   (　) in the arm, he could not write.
3. {After I had finished my homework, I took a bath.
   (　) (　) my homework, I took a bath.
4. {He sat in the chair crossing his legs.
   He sat in the chair with his legs (　).

C. 次の日本文を英文に直しなさい。（3.、4.は分詞構文を用いて）

1. 彼は私を長いこと待たせました。

2. 彼は作文を国語の先生に直してもらった。

3. 私の家は丘の上にあるので見晴らしがよいです。

4. 返事が来なかったので、彼は彼女に再度手紙を書きました。

Exercises

D. 次の英文を読み、それに続く質問に英語で答えなさい。

International Understanding

Today, we live in an increasingly close-knit international society. The nations of the world are becoming more and more interdependent, especially when it comes to exchanges of products and services. This "globalization" is being realized by highly improved communication and transportation systems. The world is definitely shrinking.

At the same time, however, many parts of the world are still troubled by conflicts and disputes, some of which develop into violence and open warfare. Why do such conflicts occur? Some have something to do with differences in political and economic systems. Others are caused by religious differences: people cannot accept or tolerate the gods that other people worship. Still others are tribal or territorial in nature.

Considering the obvious importance of friendly coexistence and maintaining good relations with one another, we must find new ways to promote mutual understanding among the peoples of the world. One of the best ways to do this is to increase the number of educational exchanges, especially of high school and university students. Young people have the ability to accept things as they are. They have the capacity to look at things without filtering them through narrow bias and prejudice. This potential for open-mindedness can easily develop into empathy for other people and their circumstances. Thus, such educational exchanges represent our best hope for fostering greater international understanding.

No.1 What are the nations of the world becoming?

No.2 How is globalization being realized?

No.3 What still troubles many parts of the world?

No.4 What is one of the best ways to promote mutual understanding among the peoples of the world?

No.5 Why are young people suited for educational exchanges?

Chapter 15-1

動名詞（1）

1. 文の主要素（主語、目的語、補語）

1) **Seeing** is **believing**.
2) **Playing** tennis is a lot of fun.
3) My hobby is **collecting** stamps.
4) He finished **washing** his car.
5) Her brother stopped **smoking** two months ago.
   - Cf. I stopped **to smoke**.（修飾語）
6) I like **swimming**.
   - Cf. I like **to swim**.（「～したい」と一時的な場合もある）
7) **It** is no use **crying** over spilt milk.（It = crying...）

2. 前置詞の目的語

8) We usually begin class by **reviewing** the last lesson.
9) How about **going** on a picnic?
10) I'm looking forward to **seeing** you soon.

3. 名詞を修飾 …「名詞 for 動名詞」と解釈

11) This is a **sleeping** car.（= a car for sleeping）
12) He happened to meet her in the **waiting** room.
13) She got a can of orange juice from the **vending** machine.

4. 動名詞を目的語にとる動詞

14) You should **practice speaking** English every day..
15) I **missed watching** the TV program last night.
16) He **suggested playing** outside.
    = He suggested that we should play outside.
    ※ 他に、admit, avoid, enjoy, escape, finish, mind, put off, stop など

Exercises

A. （　）内に入る適語を下の語群から選び、正しい形にして書き入れなさい。
1. They enjoyed (   ) a baseball game on TV.
2. There is no (   ) room in this building. Smoke outside, please.
3. Her job is (   ) vegetables.
4. She is good at (   ) the guitar.
5. My son went out without (   ) good-bye.
    [play, say, sell, smoke, watch]

B. 次の英文を日本文に直しなさい。
1. Writing a letter in English is not easy.

2. My brother's hobby is making model planes.

3. She is proud of working with the famous architect.

4. Doing nothing is doing ill.

5. We played catch without using gloves.

C. 次の日本文を英文に直しなさい。
1. トムは食堂に入って行きました。

2. 私は夕食前に宿題をし終えました。

3. 彼女はあなたから便りをもらうことを楽しみに待っています。

4. 私たちは彼女が部屋に入って来たとき、話をやめました。

5. 彼女は人形を作るのが得意です。

Exercises

D. 次の英文を読み、No.1, 2, 4は書き出しに続けるのに最も適切なものを、No.3は質問に対する最も適切な答を選びなさい。

Travel in Comfort

Traveling around the country is one of my favorite pastimes. I love visiting fascinating new places and meeting all kinds of interesting people. I used to travel from place to place by plane. But not any longer. These days I do most of my traveling by car. Let me tell you why.

During one flight from Seattle to Chicago, I was enjoying reading a guidebook with my overhead reading light on. Now, as you know, airplane seats are too cramped for comfort. Passengers are forced to sit so close together! Anyway, my reading light was bothering the man in the seat next to me. He kept looking over at me and frowning. So I put away my book, turned out my light, and fell fast asleep. Since then, as I said, I seldom go anywhere by airplane. I drive everywhere. It takes longer, but it is so much more fun and comfortable. Besides, no one bothers me, and I don't bother anyone, either.

Note: cramped：狭苦しい、窮屈な

No.1 One of the writer's pleasures is
  (a) visiting famous people.
  (b) reading books.
  (c) taking trips.

No.2 The writer thinks that traveling by airplane is
  (a) less troublesome.
  (b) uncomfortable.
  (c) more fun.

No.3 What made the writer give up traveling by airplane?
  (a) An unpleasant experience.
  (b) He bought a new car.
  (c) The high prices.

No.4 Now the writer's favorite way to travel is
  (a) walking.
  (b) driving.
  (c) by train.

Chapter 15-2 動名詞（2）

1. 動名詞の意味上の主語
  1) Do you mind **my closing** the window?
     = Do you mind if I close the window?
  2) I am sure of **your being** a good boy.
  3) She complained of **her husband coming** home late.

2. 完了動名詞 … 述語動詞の「時」より以前の「時」を表す
  4) She scolded me for **having eaten** all the cakes.
  5) I regret **not having come** to you.
  6) He is proud of **my having passed** the examination.

3. 目的語が動名詞の場合と不定詞の場合とでは意味が異なる動詞
  7) I **remember watching** that movie.
     Cf. Please **remember to lock** the door.
  8) I shall never **forget hearing** his lecture.
     Cf. Don't **forget to buy** the magazine for me.
  9) He **tried eating** some raw fish. 「試しに～してみる」
     Cf. He **tried to eat** some raw fish. 「～しようと努める」
     ※ 他に、like, hate, love, regret など

4. 受身の意味を持つ動名詞
  10) My shoes **need mending**. ［= to be mended］
  11) This book is **worth reading**.

5. その他
  12) I don't **feel like studying** at all.
  13) **On hearing** the news, she turned pale.
      = As soon as she heard the news, she turned pale.
  14) You cannot be too careful **in crossing** the street.
      = You cannot be too careful when you cross the street.
  15) **There is no accounting** for tastes.
      = It is impossible to account for tastes.
  16) I **cannot help wondering** at your impudence.
      = I cannot but wonder at your impudence.
  17) **It goes without saying that** she is an excellent pianist.
      = It is needless to say that ［Needless to say,］ she is an excellent pianist.
  18) This is a picture **of his own painting**.
      = This is a picture which he himself painted.

Exercises

A. 次の各組の文の意味が同じになるように（　）内に適語を入れなさい。

1. { Whenever I see this picture, I think of my mother.
   I never see this picture (　　) (　　) of my mother.

2. { How about making trip to Europe this summer?
   What do you (　　) to (　　) a trip to Europe this summer?

3. { He could not attend the meeting because he was ill.
   Illness prevented him (　　) (　　) the meeting.

B. 次の各組の英文を下線部に注意して日本文に直しなさい。

1. { a. I remember <u>turning</u> off the light.
   b. Please remember <u>to turn</u> off the light.

2. { a. I regret <u>saying</u> that he died of cancer.
   b. I regret <u>to say</u> that he died of cancer.

3. { a. Would you mind <u>opening</u> the window?
   b. Would you mind <u>my opening</u> the window?

C. 次の日本文を動名詞を用いて英文に直しなさい。

1. 彼は京都に着くとすぐに彼女に会いに行きました。

2. 彼女が重病から回復する見込みはありません。

3. その事実を否定することはできません。

Exercises

D. 次の英文を読み、それに続く質問に英語で答えなさい。

To Your Health

Young people often do not realize how important it is to be in good health, nor do they know much about health management and maintenance. This is partly because they simply do not have sufficient knowledge about health and medical matters. Another reason is that they have never suffered from a serious illness or been hospitalized. As an old saying goes, you don't realize how important health is until you lose it. So young people tend to take health for granted. They overlook the daily care of their body and mind. They eat too much, drink excessively, and smoke too many cigarettes. Nor do they get enough exercise. And other than the compulsory routine health check-up at school, they seldom go to the doctor to make sure everything is in good working order.

This lifestyle can cause all kinds of health problems over the long run. Excessive eating and drinking can develop into the so-called "metabolic syndrome," which can lead to obesity, diabetes, and heart disease. Smoking can cause various types of cancer, lung cancer in particular. Lack of exercise can bring on high blood pressure and damage the blood vessels, which gradually increases the risk of heart attack and stroke.

We know that ignoring health management and maintenance has dire consequences. Now, we must make sure that our young people are aware of the importance of health—before they lose it for good.

No.1 What don't young people often realize?

No.2 What do young people tend to do?

No.3 What can an uncontrolled lifestyle cause over the long run?

No.4 What will happen if people smoke?

No.5 What must we do to keep our young people in good health?

Chapter 16-1
関係詞（1）

1. 関係代名詞

先行詞 \ 格	主格	所有格	目的格
人	who	whose	whom
人以外	which	whose, of which	which
何でもよい	that	—	that
なし	what	—	what

1) I have an uncle **who**［**that**］is rich.
2) I know a boy **whose** father is a pilot.
3) He is a man **whom**［**that**］I respect very much.
4) Look at the picture **which**［**that**］is on the wall.
5) The house **whose** roof［the roof **of which**］is blue is my grandfather's.
6) The question **which**［**that**］I asked him was not difficult.
8) **What** he said is true.
9) He is not **what** he was ten years ago.「10年前の彼」

2. 限定用法と継続用法

10) He has two sons **who** want to work for old people.（他にも息子がいる可能性あり）
11) He has two sons, **who** want to work for old people.（= and they）
12) He broke the window, **which** made his father angry.（= and it）

3. おもにthatが用いられる場合

13) 先行詞に最上級の形容詞、the only, the very, the first, all, no などがつくとき
    He is **the richest** man **that** I know.
    Mr. Yoshino is **the only** person **that** supports me here.
    This is **the very** picture **that** I have long wanted to see.（まさにその）
    The first student **that** answered the difficult question was my rival.
14) 人と人以外が同時に先行詞になっている場合
    Look at **the boy and the dog that** are playing over there.

4. 関係代名詞の省略

15) Tom has several people（**whom**）he has to help.（目的格）
16) This is the bag（**which**）she bought yesterday.（目的格）
17) There is somebody（**that**）wants to see you at the gate.（There is / are...の構文内で）
18) This is the best book（**that**）there is on the subject.（直後にthere is / areが続く場合）
19) He is not the man（**that**）he was ten years ago.（be動詞の補語）

Exercises

A. 次の二つの文を関係代名詞を使って一つの文に書き換えなさい。
1. Tanaka is a college student.　He lives in Tokyo.
2. The man was Columbus.　He discovered America.
3. The girl is my sister.　You met her yesterday.
4. I have a friend.　Her mother is a famous pianist.
5. This is the first letter.　I have received it from my father.

B. 次の文中の（　）内に適当な関係代名詞を入れなさい。
1. They are the students（　　　）arrived here just now.
2. The mountain（　　　）top is covered with snow is Mt. Fuji.
3. This is the very book（　　　）I have wanted to read.
4. A car ran over the old man and his dog（　　　）were crossing the road.
5. I will lend you this book,（　　　）you will find interesting.

C. 次の英文を日本文に直しなさい。
1. He gave me all the books that he had.
2. He was the only boy that could answer the question.
3. Tell me the name of the horse which won the race.
4. The building which you see over there is our college.
5. I remained silent, which seemed to irritate him.

D. 次の日本文を関係代名詞を用いて英文に直しなさい。
1. パリは誰もが訪れたいと思っている都市のひとつです。

2. これは私が今まで読んだうちで一番面白い本です。

3. 私は英語の得意な学生を何人か知っています。

4. 表紙の青い本が私のものです。

5. 彼女には娘が三人いるが、三人とも医者です。

Exercises

E. 次の英文を読み、それに続く質問にNo.1, 3は英語で答え、No.2は質問に対する最も適切な答を、No.4は書き出しに続けるのに最も適切なものを選びなさい。

Instant Ramen

The history of instant "ramen" noodles is more interesting than you might expect. Momofuku Ando was the owner and operator of a small food company. It was his dream to create an instant food product that would be healthy and easy to make. He experimented for years and finally came up with instant ramen. All you had to do was add boiling water, cover for three minutes, and enjoy.

Mr. Ando eventually changed the name of his company to Nissin Foods. The first instant noodle dish the company introduced was called "Chicken Ramen." At first, it was a luxury item that cost six times as much as fresh "udon" noodles. But Chicken Ramen was an instant success, so to speak. Many other companies were soon making and selling similar products. Before long, competition had brought the price down. So today, instant ramen is not only quick and easy to make, but it is also cheap.

No.1 Who invented instant ramen noodles?

No.2 How long should a person wait before he / she eats instant ramen noodles?
  (a) Ten minutes.
  (b) Five minutes.
  (c) Three minutes.

No.3 What was Nissin Foods' first instant ramen called?

No.4 When the first instant ramen was put on the market,
  (a) it was very expensive.
  (b) it was not a success.
  (c) it was similar to other products.

Chapter 16-2 関係詞（2）

1. 関係代名詞と前置詞
1) This is the computer **about which** I spoke the other day.（文語）
2) This is the computer（**which**）I spoke **about** the other day.（口語）

2. 関係代名詞の二重制限
3) There is no one（**that**）I know **that** can run faster than Ben.

3. as, but, than の用法
4) This is **such** an easy book **as** anyone can read.
5) There is **no** man **but** loves［that doesn't love］his own country.
6) He gave me **more** money **than** was expected.

4. 関係副詞
7) I know the day **when** she was born.（時）
    Cf. He came home at seven, **when** we were having dinner.（= and then）
8) That is the house **where** my uncle lives.（場所）
    Cf. We went to Australia, **where** we stayed for a week.（= and there）
9) Do you know the reason **why** she got angry?（理由）
10) This is **how**［**the way**］I did it.（方法）

5. 関係形容詞
11) I gave the poor woman **what**（little）money I had.「（少ないながらも）すべての」

6. 複合関係詞
12) whoever, whichever, whatever など
    I will invite **whoever**［**anyone who**］wants to come.
13) whenever, wherever, however
    Whenever I call him up, he is not at home.

7. what や as を含む慣用表現
14) He is **what we call**［**what is called**］a walking dictionary.「いわゆる」
15) Leaves **are to** the plant **what** lungs **are to** the animal.「A is to B what C is to D. → AのBに対する関係は、CのDに対する関係と同じ」
16) A man's worth lies not in **what he has** but in **what he is**.「財産」と「人柄」
17) My parents have made me **what I am today**.「今日の私」
18) She is beautiful, **what is better**, intelligent.「さらによいことには」
19) What with the wind and（**what with**）the rain, they gave up going out.「～やら…やらで」
20) **As is often the case with** Roy, he was late for school.「～にはよくあることだが」
21) **As was to be expected**, they lost the game.「予測されたとおり」

Exercises

A. （　）内に入る適語を下の語群から選び、書き入れなさい。

1. Give the book to （　　） wants it.
2. He is handsome, and （　　） is better, very kind.
3. You may invite （　　） you like.
4. Who （　　） has a great deal of self-respect could stand such an insult?
5. Let children read such books （　　） will make them better and wiser.

　　　［as,　what,　that,　whoever,　whomever］

B. 次の英文を日本文に直しなさい。

1. That is why I don't want you to go swimming.

2. Whoever may say so, I would never believe him.

3. I gave her what little money I had.

4. Help yourself to whatever food there is in the refrigerator.

5. As is often the case with him, he left his umbrella somewhere yesterday.

C. 次の日本文を関係代名詞を用いて英文に直しなさい。

1. どちらでも欲しいものを取りなさい。

2. あなたが来たいときにいつでもお会いいたします。

3. 私が今日あるのは母のおかげです。

4. 前に犯したのと同じ間違いをしてはいけません。

Exercises

D. 次の英文を読み、それに続く質問に英語で答えなさい。

Endless War

Is there any country in the world that doesn't have an armed force? I don't think so. Advanced industrial nations in particular have very advanced military forces. These nations even compete against each other to see who can build up the most powerful army, navy, and air force, to see who can come up with the most destructive weapons, including nuclear arms. Some nations form military alliances and conduct "collective defense" drills to protect themselves from their common enemies, who, meanwhile, form such collective defense alliances of their own. It sometimes seems as if this perpetual military competition is an "endless war" in itself.

Why does this military expansion continue? Is it because countries can't trust each other and are afraid of being attacked and invaded? Or is it simply because a strong military satisfies national pride and dignity?

Whatever the precise reason may be, it's time we stopped this military expansion. We need to shift our attention to the growing phenomena of international economic interdependence and globalization. To paraphrase an old saying, no nation is an island. These days, we all need and depend on each other. At the same time, we face various worldwide problems—global warming, for example, and the AIDS epidemic. These problems cannot be solved without the cooperative efforts of all nations. The time has come for us to devote our energies to finding ways to live in harmony rather than to finding ways to outdo others in military might. It's time to end this endless war.

No.1 What do advanced industrial nations have?
No.2 What does perpetual military competition seem like?
No.3 What do we need to shift our attention to?
No.4 What are some examples of worldwide problems?
No.5 What do we need to do to end endless war?

Chapter 17-1

仮定法（1）

1. 法
1) 直説法（事実をありのままに述べる）
   He **is** a doctor.
2) 命令法（相手に対して命令したり、依頼したりする）
   Open the window.
3) 仮定法（事実と反対のことを仮定または想像、願望して述べる）
   If I **were** free now, I **would** go with you.

2. 直説法のIf-節 … 単なる条件
4) If it is fine tomorrow, we will go on a picnic.
5) If you climbed that mountain yesterday, you must have had a good sleep last night.
6) If you have visited the museum many times, I'm sure you know it well.

3. 仮定法過去（1）… 現在の事実に反する仮定
   If…{(助)動詞の過去形; **were / was**}, …{**would, should, could, might**}＋原形
7) If I **had** time, I **would call** on you.
   = As I don't have time, I won't call on you.
8) If I **were** rich, I **could buy** a yacht.
   = As I am not rich, I cannot buy a yacht.
9) If he **could** play soccer as well as you do, he **would join** the club.
   = As he cannot play soccer as well as you do, he won't join the club.

4. 仮定法過去完了（1）… 過去の事実に反する仮定
   If…{**had**＋過去分詞}, …{**would, should, could, migh**}＋**have**＋過去分詞
10) If she **had had** enough money, she **would have bought** the dress.
    = As she didn't have enough money, she didn't buy the dress.
11) If he **had worked** hard, he **would have passed** the exam.
    = As he didn't work hard, he didn't pass the exam.

5. Ifの省略（仮定法過去の場合は、ふつう、動詞がwereかhadに限られる）
12) **Were I** a bird, I would fly to you soon.
    = **If I were** a bird, I would fly to you soon.
13) **Should it** rain on the way, we will turn back.
    = **If it should** rain on the way, we will turn back.
14) **Had you taken** my advice, you would have succeeded.
    = **If you had taken** my advice, you would have succeeded.

Exercises

A. 次の英文の（　　）内から適当な語句を選びなさい。
1. He will help you if he (has, had, had had) time.
2. If my father (is, are, were) alive, I could go to college.
3. If I (have, had, had had) the money, I could have bought that guitar.
4. If you did your best, you (could succeed, had succeeded, could have succeeded).

B. 次の英文を仮定法を用いて書き換えなさい。
1. As the girl is weak, she can't walk all the way with us.

2. He is so old that he can't run so fast as you.

3. He did not work hard, so he failed in the examination.

4. As it was raining yesterday, we could not go on a picnic.

C. 次の各組の文が同じ意味になるように（　）内に適語を入れなさい。
1. { As I am not so young as you, I cannot play football.
   { If I (　　) as young as you, I (　　) play football.
2. { I could not write a longer letter because I didn't have more time.
   { I could (　　) (　　) a longer letter if I (　　) had more time.
3. { Should you change your mind, nobody would blame you.
   { (　　) (　　) (　　) change your mind, nobody would blame you.

D. 次の日本文を英文に直しなさい。
1. 車があれば、あなたをドライブに連れて行ってあげるのですが。

2. 彼がもっと注意深ければ、同じ間違いはしないでしょう。

3. もし君が7時に家を出ていたら、電車に乗れたのに。

Exercises

E. 次の英文を読み、それに続く質問では、それぞれの書き出しに続けるのに最も適切なものを選びなさい。

Culture Shock

Say you are living in London. All of a sudden you begin to hate the fish and chips that at first you have been happy to eat practically every day. Or maybe you have been going to school in the United States and suddenly begin to miss Japanese rice and your mother's homemade miso soup. That's what culture shock can do to you.

Our native culture is like a cocoon of comfort and security. When we live outside of this cocoon for a while, we sometimes react sensitively because we are separated from the familiar things that make us feel at ease. When this happens, many people jump on the first flight back home. But if we know why this is happening to us, we don't need to take such drastic action. We can do something that gives us back our feeling of safety and comfort. Take my American friend here in Tokyo, for example. Whenever he feels a bout of culture shock coming on, he heads for McDonald's and orders a Big Mac.

Notes: cocoon：居心地のいい場所、コクーン　a bout of：ひとしきりの〜、〜の発作

No.1 "Fish and chips" is a famous fast food in
　　　(a) England.　(b) India.　(c) China.

No.2 Our native culture makes us feel
　　　(a) nervous.　(b) safe.　(c) sad.

No.3 When we live overseas, we sometimes
　　　(a) lose our way easily.
　　　(b) respond emotionally.
　　　(c) feel at ease.

No.4 When the writer's American friend experiences culture shock,
　　　(a) he flies back to the United States.
　　　(b) he goes back to his house in Japan.
　　　(c) he eats a hamburger at a hamburger shop.

Chapter 17-2

仮定法（2）

1. 仮定法過去・過去完了（2）… 現在あるいは過去の事実に反する願望

1) I **wish**（= **If only**）I **could** speak English.
   = I am sorry I cannot speak English.
2) I **would rather** you **were** here today.
3) **If only**（= I wish）I **had asked** her about that.
   = I am sorry I didn't ask her about that.

2. If…should（条件）と If … were to（仮定）

4) If I **should** fail, I would try again.
5) If it **should** rain tomorrow, I will stay at home.
6) If you **should** meet Ken during your stay in Boston, say hello to him.
7) If the sun **were to rise** in the west, he **would not change** his mind.
8) If your beloved dog **were to disappear** today, what **would** you **do**?

3. 仮定法を含む慣用表現

9) **If it were not for** his idleness, he would be a good student.
10) **If it had not been for** your help, I could not have accomplished it.
11) He speaks English **as if** he **were**（was や is の場合もある）an American.
12) She looks **as if** she **had seen** a ghost.
13) He is, **as it were**, a walking dictionary.
14) **It is time** you **went** to bed.
15) I **would like to** live here.
16) **Would you like** some coffee?
17) **Would you mind** opening the window?
18) You **had better** not sit up late at night.

4. If -節のない仮定法

19) **A member of our club would never do** such a thing.
    = If he/she were a member of our club, he/she would never do such a thing.
20) **But for** your help, I **could not have finished** my report by the deadline.
    = If it had not been for your help, I **could not have finished** ….
21) **Without** you, we **couldn't carry out** our plan.
    = If it were not for you, we couldn't carry out our plan.
22) **To hear** him talk, you **would take** him for me.
    = If you heard him talk, you would take him for me.
23) The same thing, **happening** in Japan, **would cause** a panic.
    = The same thing, if it happened in Japan, would cause a panic.

Exercises

A. 次の英文を日本文に直しなさい。

1. I would rather you made friends with them.

2. To hear him speak English, you would take him for an American.

3. A man of common sense could not do such a thing.

B. 次の各組の文がほぼ同じ意味になるように（　）内に適語を入れなさい。

1. { I am sorry I am not as beautiful as she.
   I (　　) (　　) (　　) as beautiful as she.

2. { If he had seen you, he would have been delighted.
   (　　) (　　) (　　) you, he would have been delighted.

3. { If he had not followed my advice, he would have failed.
   He followed my advice;(　　) he would have failed.

4. { If it had not been for your help, I could not have finished the work.
   (　　) your help, I could not have finished the work.

5. { A wise mother would be stricter with her sons.
   (　　) she (　　) a wise mother, she would be stricter with her sons.

C. 次の日本文を英文に直しなさい。

1. そろそろ学校へ行く時間よ。

2. 高校でもっと英語を勉強しておけばよかったなあ。

3. 彼女はまるで幽霊でも見たかのような顔つきだった。

4. 自動車がなければこの通りももっと静かなんですが。

5. 夜はひとりで外出しない方がいいよ。

Exercises

D. 次の英文を読み、それに続く質問に英語で答えなさい。

Community Bonds

No one can live alone. This fact is something that we need to reconsider and reaffirm in our daily lives. In Japan, in the not too distant past, we supported each other in our neighborhoods and places of work. We knew who the members of our community were, and participated in collective activities such as planting rice and assisting each other at weddings and funerals. At work, we went on company trips with our colleagues or took part in company sports events. Nowadays, however, things have changed dramatically. Often, we have no idea who lives right next door. We tend to avoid becoming acquainted with our neighbors and spending time with them. If this trend towards "social isolation" continues, what will our lives be like? Couldn't we eventually find ourselves living as if on a lonely island, cut off from the rest of the world?

What brought about this change? It may have something to do with the stage of economic development we have reached and the subsequent changes this has brought to our values and attitudes. During the 1950s and 1960s, we were relatively poor, and being poor, we needed each other to survive. In those days, we were still quite collectivistic; we cared about other people and valued even seemingly useless "junk." But as our economy grew in the 1970s and 1980s, we became more individualistic. We valued our personal needs more highly, and began paying less attention to what others were doing and needed. We also indulged ourselves in excessive consumption.

It may seem as if our lives are better today, but are they really? Haven't we lost the community bonds that once held us together, and become more lonely and helpless in the process? Don't we need to return to our old values and the practice of looking out for one another?

No.1 What did we used to do in our neighborhoods and places of work?

No.2 How have things changed nowadays?

No.3 What has changed our values and attitudes?

No.4 What were Japanese like during the 1950s and 1960s?

No.5 Where do we need to return to?

Chapter 18-1 時制の一致・話法（1）

1. 時制の一致

1) She **says** that she **is** happy. → She **said** that she **was** happy.
2) I **believe** that they **are** honest. → I **believed** that they **were** honest.
3) I **think** that she **was** ill. → I **thought** that she **had been** ill.
4) It **seems** that he **sold** the house. → It **seemed** that he **had sold** the house.

※ 時制の一致の例外（不変の真理、現在の習慣など）

5) The teacher **says** that the earth **moves** around the sun.（不変の真理）
　→ The teacher **said** that the earth **moves** around the sun.
6) She **says** that she **goes** to bed at ten every night.（現在の習慣）
　→ She **said** that she **goes** to bed at ten every night.
7) He **teaches** us that Columbus **discovered** America.（歴史上の事実）
　→ He **taught** us that Columbus **discovered** America.
8) I **wish** I **had** a yacht.（仮定法）
　→ I **wished** I **had** a yacht.

2. 話法の転換（1）…（直接話法）→（間接話法）

※ 平叙文

9) He said, "**I am** busy." → He said **that he was** busy.
10) He said, "It **will** rain **tomorrow**." → He said **that** it **would** rain **the next day**.
11) She **said to** me, "**I am** glad to see **you**."
　→ She **told** me **that she was** glad to see **me**.
12) She **said to** me, "**I went** to the zoo **yesterday**."
　→ She **told** me **that she had gone** to the zoo **the day before**.
13) He **said to** me, "**I saw this** boy **here** a week **ago**."
　→ He **told** me **that he had seen that** boy **there** a week **before**.

※ 疑問文

14) She **said to** him, "**Do you like this** book?"
　→ She **asked** him **if**［**whether**］ he **liked that** book.
15) I **said to myself**, "**Will** she be at home **tonight**?"
　→ I **wondered if** she **would** be at home **that night**.
16) He **said to** me, "Where **is my** bag?"
　→ He **asked** me where **his** bag **was**.
17) I **said to** him, "Who **went** with **you**?"
　→ I **asked** him who **had gone** with **him**.

Exercises

A. 次の各文の下線部を過去時制にして全文を書き換えなさい。
1. He <u>doesn't know</u> that the Civil War broke out in 1861.
2. I <u>hear</u> that he moved to the United Kingdom.
3. He <u>says</u> that he goes to school before eight every day.
4. He <u>thinks</u> that the sun moves round the earth.

B. 次の英文の（　）内に適語を入れなさい。
1. I asked him （　　） he could swim.
2. Father （　　） me why I had been late for school.
3. My uncle told me that he （　　）（　　） to Europe twice.
4. He told me that he （　　） come to see me the next day.

C. 次の英文の誤りを訂正しなさい。
1. The boy didn't know that Cuba was an island country.
2. My little daughter answered that four and three were seven.
3. The other day he told me that he has seen me three years ago.
4. The teacher asked me when World War II had ended.

D. 次の英文の話法を変えなさい。
1. He said, "I saw this man long ago."

2. I said to her, "When did you buy it?"

3. He said to her, "Can you play the piano?"

4. Mary said that her mother was free that day.

5. She asked him if he would buy her a new dress.

6. He told me that he didn't understand what I said.

E. 次の日本文を直接、間接話法の二通りの英文に直しなさい。
1. 「明日は雨だろう」と彼は言いました。

2. 彼は私に「君にこれをやってもらいたい」と言いました。

3. 「7年前はどこに住んでいたのですか」と彼女は私に尋ねました。

Exercises

F. 次の英文を読み、それに続く質問にNo.1は英語で答えなさい。他はそれぞれの書き出しに続けるのに最も適切なものを選びなさい。

Michael J. Fox and Parkinson's Disease

When Michael J. Fox was first diagnosed with Parkinson's disease, he kept it a secret from the public. One of the symptoms of the disease is body shaking. By 1998, Michael's shaking had become so severe that he realized he could no longer hide it, especially when acting. So he decided to make a public announcement. He also wrote his autobiography, the profits from which were used to set up a foundation to fight the disease. Michael's declaration and book have changed the lives of millions of Parkinson's sufferers. Take Barbara Smith, for example. One day Barbara, a big fan of Michael's, was standing at the cash register at a store. Suddenly, her hand started shaking. The clerk was concerned and asked her what was wrong with her. When Barbara told him she had Parkinson's disease, the clerk said, "Oh, just like Michael J. Fox." It was the first time she had not felt embarrassed by her disease.

Notes: diagnose：診断する　the profits from which：それから得られた利益

No.1 When did Michael J. Fox announce his Parkinson's disease?

No.2 A person with Parkinson's disease
　(a) shakes.
　(b) cannot speak fluently.
　(c) has severe headaches.

No.3 Michael J. Fox wrote his autobiography
　(a) to get rich.
　(b) to make a movie from.
　(c) to establish a foundation.

No.4 When Barbara's hand started shaking, the clerk said to her,
　(a) "What was wrong with her?"
　(b) "What is wrong with her?"
　(c) "What was wrong with you?"
　(d) "What is wrong with you?"

Chapter 18-2

時制の一致・話法（2）

1. 話法の転換（2）…（直接話法）→（間接話法）

※ 命令文

1) I **said to** him, "**Do your** best." → I **told** him **to do his** best.
2) My wife **said to** me, "**Don't** wake up the baby."
   → My wife **told** me **not to** wake up the baby.
3) He **said to** me, "**Please** sit down." → He **asked** me **to** sit down.
4) He **said to** me, "**Let's** go home."
   → He **proposed** [**suggested**] **to** me **that we**（**should**）go home.

※ 感嘆文

5) He **said**, "What a beautiful sight it is!"
   → He **exclaimed** what a beautiful sight it was.
6) She said, "**Alas**! How careless I am!"
   → She exclaimed **with regret** that she was very careless.
7) He said, "**May** God help me!"
   → He **prayed that** God **might** help him.

※ 重文

8) He said, "**I am** rich, but I am not happy."
   → He said **that he was** rich **but that he was** not happy.
9) She **said to** me, "Get up right away, **or your meal will** get cold."
   → She **told** me **to** get up right away **or my meal would** get cold.
10) He **said to** me, "**Work harder, and you will** succeed in **your** business."
    → He **told** me that **I would** succeed in **my** business **if I worked harder**.

※ 複文

11) He said, "**I will** go on a picnic if it **is** fine **tomorrow**."
    → He said **that he would** go on a picnic if it **was** fine **the next day**.
12) She **said to** me, "What **are you going** to do after the exams **end**?"
    → She **asked** me what **I was going** to do after the exams **ended**.

※ その他の例

13) He **said to** me, "You look tired. **What did you do?**"
    → He **told** me that I looked tired and **asked** me **what I had done**.
14) The salesclerk **said to** me, "Please come in and look around. There **are** lots of discounted goods." → The salesclerk **invited** me to come in and look around, **saying** [and said] that there **were** lots of discounted goods.

Exercises

A. 次の英文の話法を変えなさい。

1. He said, "I wish I were a bird."
2. He suggested that we should go to the park.
3. She told him not to go fishing that day.
4. I asked him what had become of his sister.
5. John said to me, "If it rains, don't expect me."

B. 次の各組の文が同じ意味になるように（　）内に適語を入れなさい。

1. { The doctor said to me, "Don't go out today."
   { The doctor (　) me (　) (　) go out (　) (　).

2. { He said to her, "Please bring me some hot water."
   { He (　) her (　) bring (　) some hot water.

3. { She said, "I feel chilly. I may have caught cold."
   { She said that (　) (　) chilly and (　) (　) (　) have caught cold.

4. { He said to us, "Let's sing together."
   { He (　) to us that (　) (　) sing together.

C. 日本文と同じ意味の英文になるように、（　）内の語句を並べ替えなさい。

1. なるべく早く帰りなさいと私は彼女に言った。
   I (as soon as, told, her, she, could, come back, to).

2. あなたはいつからご病気ですかと彼は私に尋ねた。
   He (how, sick, I, asked, been, long, me, had).

3. 雪が降っているが、私は出かけると彼女は言った。
   She (that, that, she, go, was, but, would, snowing, said, it).

D. 次の日本文を直接、間接話法の二通りの英文に直しなさい。

1. 「ラジオを聴いているので騒がないで」と母は彼に言いました。

2. 「彼は外出をしていますが、間もなく帰ってくるでしょう」と彼女は私に言いました。

3. 「あなたは英語がお上手ね。どのくらい英語を勉強していらっしゃいますか」と彼女は私に言いました。

Exercises

E. 次の英文を読み、それに続く質問に英語で答えなさい。

Finding Your Future Career

One of the most difficult things for most people in life is to find the career that best suits their abilities and personality. Unless we have a very special talent in a certain field, or are strongly motivated towards a certain goal, most of us have to struggle to find our way to the right career path. But there are a few simple steps you can take to get yourself heading in the right direction.

The first step is to conduct a thorough self-analysis. This means asking yourself questions like, "What do I most enjoy doing?" or "What am I most interested in?" The next step is to make up a list of occupations and professions that correspond to your preferences and interests. The third step is to compare the vocations you have selected from a variety of standpoints, including job content, social function, and income level. The final step is to settle on the career that best satisfies your personal needs.

While following these steps can go a long way towards helping you find the career that best fits your requirements, another effective way is to actually get out and experience many different jobs and to see as many different worlds as you can. A middle-aged professional, speaking at a university-sponsored career-planning session, once told his audience that he had learned as much outside the campus as he had inside. "You can analyze and test yourself," he said, "by trying all sorts of part-time jobs, and you can broaden your horizons by meeting and listening to lots of different people." College students are lucky in that they can have a variety of part-time jobs as long as those jobs do not interfere with their academic studies. Adding these little "side trips" to your itinerary should help you find the career path that will lead you most successfully and happily through life.

No.1 What do most of us have to struggle to do?
No.2 What do we need to do first to find a suitable career?
No.3 How do we make the final decision in our career choice?
No.4 What is another good way to find an appropriate career?
No.5 What must college students not let their part-time jobs do?

Let's Enjoy English

Copyright © 2008

Tetsuzo Sato
Yuji Sato
Tatsuya Aramaki
Kenji Ikeda
Fumio Mouri

All Rights Reserved
No part of this book may be reproduced in any form without written permission from the authors and Nan'un-do Co., Ltd.

著作権法上、無断複写・複製は禁じられています。

Let's Enjoy English [B-595]
大学生ための総合英語

1 刷	2008年1月25日
10 刷	2017年2月25日

著 者	佐藤哲三	Tetsuzo Sato
	佐藤勇治	Yuji Sato
	荒巻龍也	Tatsuya Aramaki
	池田賢治	Kenji Ikeda
	毛利史生	Fumio Mouri

発行者　南雲一範　Kazunori Nagumo
発行所　株式会社　南雲堂
〒162-0801　東京都新宿区山吹町361
NAN'UN-DO Publishing Co., Ltd.
361 Yamabuki-cho, Shinjuku-ku, Tokyo 162-0801, Japan
振替口座：00160-0-46863
TEL: 03-3268-2311（代表）／FAX: 03-3269-2486
編集者　TA

製版所	啓文堂
装　丁	Nスタジオ
検　印	省　略
コード	ISBN9784-523-17595-7 C0082

Printed in Japan

E-mail　nanundo@post.email.ne.jp
URL　http://www.nanun-do.co.jp